Inclusion and Belonging in Cities of Tomorrow

"The rapid spread of smart cities around the world has the potential to deepen inequality and accelerate inclusion and belonging. In his powerful and timely new volume, Dr. Victor Pineda calls on city leaders and residents to adopt a radically inclusive approach to urban design in a digitally transforming world. Drawing on lived experience and deep research, *Inclusion and Belonging in Cities of Tomorrow* is an invitation to re-imagine the twenty-first century city. Its central message is provocative and persuasive: the proactive embrace of marginalized communities in the design and decision-making of cities is key to improving governance, competitiveness, sustainability, and quality of life for all."
 —Robert Muggah, *Smart city expert and TED speaker, Founder of SecDev and Igarape Institute, Author of Terra Incognita (Random House)*

"Victor Pineda's book is a seminal contribution to the field of urban governance and design. By highlighting the importance of inclusion and access in city planning, he challenges conventional notions and inspires readers to reimagine the future of our cities. 'Inclusion and Belonging in Cities of Tomorrow' is a thought-provoking and empowering read that calls for transformative change, inviting policymakers, planners, scholars and activists to work together in creating cities that prioritize the well-being and participation of all residents."
 —Eugenie L. Birch, FAICP, *Nussdorf Professor of Urban Research, Department of City and Regional Planning, Dean, Graduate Studies, Stuart Weitzman School of Design*

"Dr. Victor Pineda's vision of accessible, inclusive cities is not only compelling, but an essential and seminal contribution to the fields of design and governance. His book provides a thought-provoking roadmap for designers to follow, to ensure our future cities serve the diverse disabled community holistically and fully. Inclusion should not be an afterthought in design, and this book expertly highlights *why* and *how* we should begin: the task belongs not only to designers (e.g., architects, landscape architects, urban designers), but in direct partnership with policymakers, city planners, and activists working together to prioritize the participation and integration of direct feedback from stakeholders with disabilities. As a former student of Dr. Pineda, this book is a must-read for students in design and practitioners alike, who wish to become more inclusive of the disabled community and work towards designing a more accessible world."
 —Alexa Vaughn, ASLA, FAAR, *Landscape Designer, DeafScape and Accessibility Specialist, and PhD Student at UCLA*

"Victor Pineda is a powerful voice advocating for cities that are inclusive and accessible to all. This is absolutely critical to achieve the SDG target of leaving no one behind by 2030, an increasingly complex task due to the development setbacks caused by COVID, climate change and conflict. When designed and managed inclusively, cities offer an effective pathway for people to break out of the cycle of poverty and marginalization. Victor's tireless energy and ability to connect across global audiences of policymakers, development practitioners and communities is an important driving force towards sustainable urbanization."
—Sameh Wahba, *The World Bank Group*

"In 'Inclusion and Belonging in Cities of Tomorrow,' Dr. Victor Pineda presents a comprehensive and practical guide to using innovative approaches to transforming cities into spaces that embrace diversity and ensure accessibility for all. Technology should be harnessed to accelerate progress toward better inclusivity and accessibility in every city around the world. This book is an essential resource for anyone committed to creating inclusive communities and fostering a sense of belonging for every individual."
—Miguel Gamiño Jr., *Former CTO of the New York City, Chief Experience Officer and Founding Partner Simplicity*

"This book is a groundbreaking, inspiring, and urgent call for incorporating spatial justice and inclusion in urban planning and public policies. It is an important resource for understanding how older individuals and people with disabilities can be prioritized in the design and planning of cities and how everyone benefits."
—Vinit Mukhija, *Professor, Department of Urban Planning, UCLA Luskin School of Public Affairs*

"Dr. Pineda's book, 'Inclusion and Belonging in Cities of Tomorrow', is a profound contribution to our understanding of urban inclusivity. The compelling case studies and innovative frameworks align perfectly with the New Urban Agenda and my organization's contributions towards the United Nations' Sustainable Development Goals. This book is an indispensable resource for any global leader committed to building inclusive, safe, resilient, and sustainable cities."
—Maimunah Sharif, *Deputy Secretary-General United Nations, Executive Director, UN Habitat, Nairobi, Kenya*

Victor Santiago Pineda

Inclusion and Belonging in Cities of Tomorrow

Governance and Access by Design

Victor Santiago Pineda
Department of City and Regional Planning
University of California, Berkeley
Berkeley, CA, USA

ISBN 978-981-99-3855-1   ISBN 978-981-99-3856-8 (eBook)
https://doi.org/10.1007/978-981-99-3856-8

© The Editor(s) (if applicable) and The Author(s) 2024. This book is an open access publication.

Open Access This book is licensed under the terms of the Creative Commons Attribution 4.0 International License (http://creativecommons.org/licenses/by/4.0/), which permits use, sharing, adaptation, distribution and reproduction in any medium or format, as long as you give appropriate credit to the original author(s) and the source, provide a link to the Creative Commons licence and indicate if changes were made.

The images or other third party material in this book are included in the book's Creative Commons licence, unless indicated otherwise in a credit line to the material. If material is not included in the book's Creative Commons licence and your intended use is not permitted by statutory regulation or exceeds the permitted use, you will need to obtain permission directly from the copyright holder.

The use of general descriptive names, registered names, trademarks, service marks, etc. in this publication does not imply, even in the absence of a specific statement, that such names are exempt from the relevant protective laws and regulations and therefore free for general use.

The publisher, the authors, and the editors are safe to assume that the advice and information in this book are believed to be true and accurate at the date of publication. Neither the publisher nor the authors or the editors give a warranty, expressed or implied, with respect to the material contained herein or for any errors or omissions that may have been made. The publisher remains neutral with regard to jurisdictional claims in published maps and institutional affiliations.

Cover illustration: Pattern © Melisa Hasan/ Image ©Peter Hermes Furian / Alamy Stock Photo

This Palgrave Macmillan imprint is published by the registered company Springer Nature Singapore Pte Ltd.
The registered company address is: 152 Beach Road, #21-01/04 Gateway East, Singapore 189721, Singapore

Paper in this product is recyclable.

Foreword

In the rapidly urbanizing world of today, the challenges of creating sustainable, inclusive, and equitable cities are more pressing than ever. As urban populations continue to grow, the need for radically inclusive governance and design strategies to holistically address wellbeing, resilience, and belonging in cities becomes increasingly urgent.

This book offers a compelling examination of the ways in which cities can be designed and governed to foster greater inclusion and belonging for all residents. Drawing on a wide range of theoretical frameworks including phenomenology, personal experiences, and empirical research, this book explores the challenges and opportunities of creating inclusive cities in the twenty-first century. Leveraging the unique, enriched lived experience of disability provides readers with valuable insights into the human condition and the systemic failures present in historical and contemporary policy, planning, and design.

The rise of smart cities and the increasing use of technology in urban governance has the potential to either deepen existing inequalities or promote greater inclusion and belonging. This book examines how cities can design their governance and technology systems to foster inclusion and belonging, particularly for marginalized communities.

The book explores the concepts of inclusion and belonging, and how they relate to urban environments. It introduces the concept of radical inclusion and then examines how central this concept is to building just and equitable cities. Technology plays a role in how cities are governed and the potential impacts of poor urban planning, policies, and design on inclusion and belonging. This includes case studies of cities that have successfully implemented inclusive policies, governance and technology systems, as well as identifying the challenges faced for those that have struggled to do so.

The second theme woven throughout the book focuses on the role of design in fostering inclusion and belonging. This includes discussions of Universal Design, participatory design, and other design approaches that prioritize the needs of marginalized communities.

The third theme of the book is practice. What practical steps can city leaders and urban stakeholders take to advance radical inclusion? This book offers practical guidance for cities and urban leaders on how to design inclusive governance and management systems. This includes best practices for involving marginalized communities in decision-making and strategies for addressing bias and discrimination in data collection.

The closing section of the book highlights emerging trends and the crucial role that digital transformation can play in either hindering or progressing inclusion in our cities. The book concludes by considering the future of inclusion and belonging in cities and the need for ongoing attention to these issues as cities continue to evolve and incorporate new technologies.

Overall, this book offers a comprehensive examination of the intersection of inclusion, belonging, and governance in urban environments. It also points to future research and frames the responsible use of technology as a catalyst for greater inclusion. Urban planners, policymakers, and other professionals involved in designing and governing cities will find a rich set of frameworks with practical advice on how to turn theory into action. The book will also inform the emerging scholarship on urban development and digital transformation and will be of great interest to a new generation of researchers and students in urban studies and related fields.

Berkeley, CA, USA   Victor Santiago Pineda

Preface

I was born in Caracas Venezuela, a thriving and sprawling metropolis built out during the gilded age of the 1970s oil boom. Nestled in a verdant valley, Caracas beckons visitors with the tantalizing promise of tropical paradise. Towering over the bustling city, El Avila mountain serves as a constant reminder of the untamed wilderness that surrounds the concrete jungle below.

In the early 1980s, it was a place of striking contrasts: towering high-rises of opulent wealth juxtaposed against the colorful facades of shanty towns clinging precariously to hillsides. The beauty of the surrounding tropical forests was a poignant reminder of the fragility of the city's grandeur, built upon the riches of oil.

Yet, despite the chaos and the contrasts, there was one clear theme that shaped my life, inclusion. I grew up in a world, and particularly a city, that was not designed for me. I was seven years old when my physical strength began to deteriorate as my muscles began rapidly wasting away. As my muscles grew weaker, all my mother could see were the barriers that I would encounter. I oftentimes felt like I was a burden and that it was just too difficult to navigate my way through the world. Therefore, as I grew up, I was quickly forced to learn how to confront and circumvent physical, social, and institutional barriers in order to simply have a chance at living a life with dignity.

I remember how the sun would set over El Avila mountain. The city took on a new life at night, with lights twinkling in the skyscrapers casting an otherworldly glow over the city. However, Caracas had very little to offer me. In fact, it accosted me, it excluded me, it discriminated against me. My mother understood that this was not a city that would give me a fair chance. It was a city that I will never forget, with memories of its stark contrasts and heady emotions etched forever in my mind.

I write this lying in bed, with a keyboard on my chest. I use a machine to fill my lungs with air. I am a quadriplegic, and yet I am not an anomaly. The barriers I face are not barriers for me alone. Around the world, nearly a quarter of the global population faces barriers accessing their cities due to two mundane and yet embarrassingly under-studied phenomena, age or disability. Thankfully, however, this situation is now changing and it's exciting to see the field growing, thanks to a new generation of scholars and dedicated journals covering these emerging and important topics. I have written on the topic of ableism and exclusion in urban planning.[1] In Enabling Justice (2008) I argue that exclusion and ableism have been built into our cities, in both conscious and unconscious ways, for centuries. Inaccessible public spaces, inadequate transportation, and a lack of affordable, accessible housing are just a few of the ways that our built environment marginalizes disabled people. It's time for us to recognize this legacy of exclusion and work to dismantle it, by listening to the voices of disabled people and centering their needs in all aspects of urban planning and design.

The emerging literature on inclusive and accessible urban transformation highlights the importance of improving transportation networks, addressing the digital divide, leveraging technology for inclusion, and adopting multi-stakeholder approaches to create equitable and accessible urban environments for all. Studies emphasize the need for upgrading stations and interchanges (Ferrari et al. 2013),[2] ensuring digital accessibility in smart cities (Kolotouchkina et al. 2021), focusing on social indicators for inclusive urban development (Reuter 2019),[3] and including people with disabilities from the conception of smart city projects (Velasco Rico

---

[1] Victor Santiago Pineda, "Enabling Justice: Spatializing Disability in the Built Environment," Critical Planning Journal 15 (2008): 111–23.

[2] Ferrari, L., Berlingerio, M., Calabrese, F., & Reades, J. (2013). Improving the accessibility of urban transportation networks for people with disabilities. Transportation Research, 45, 27–40. https://kclpure.kcl.ac.uk/portal/files/44930309/Improving_the_Accessibility_of_Urban_Transportation_Networks_for_People_with_Disabilities.pdf

[3] Reuter, T. K. (2019). Human rights and the city: Including marginalized communities in urban development and smart cities. Journal of Human Rights, 18(4), 382–402. https://www.tandfonline.com/doi/full/10.1080/14754835.2019.1629887

2021).⁴ Other research highlights the significance of transport accessibility for social equity (Guzman et al. 2017),⁵ fostering collaboration among stakeholders (Pineda et. al. 2017),⁶ addressing mobility challenges of low-income residents and advocating for inclusive urban development policies (Pineda & Corburn 2020).⁷ This growing field offers valuable insights and guidance for promoting accessibility, equity, and inclusion in urban development.

But exclusion and inaccessible environments are not just important issues for the comparatively small number of people who, like me, live with significant or severe physical challenges, these ineffective governance and design failures affect virtually everybody. Human functioning exists on a spectrum. The spectrum of human functioning also changes and shifts with age. If you're lucky to live long enough, you will be statistically likely to acquire a disability. The demographic implications of these social changes are significant. The "gray tsunami" refers to the large aging demographic (population over the age of 60) that will contain historically unprecedented numbers of people who live with some kind of functional impairments. As medical advancements push out greater life expectancy, people with physical, sensory, or intellectual impairments are living longer and more productive lives. These demographic changes are ongoing and irreversible.

The UN Convention on the Rights of Persons with Disabilities (CRPD)⁸ acknowledges this, mandating that countries provide equal access to information, care, and medical services for persons with disabilities. But it's not just about access to services—it's about making sure that diverse and underrepresented constituents, including persons with dis-

---

⁴ Velasco Rico, C. (2021). Smart cities for all: Usability and disability bias. European Review of Digital Administration and Law, 2(1), 157–169. https://www.erdalreview.eu/free-download/979125994243212.pdf

⁵ Guzman, L. A., Oviedo, D., & Rivera, C. (2017). Assessing equity in transport accessibility to work and study: The Bogotá region. Journal of Transport Geography, 58, 236–246. https://doi.org/10.1016/j.jtrangeo.2017.01.008

⁶ Victor Santiago Pineda, Stephen Meyer, and John Paul Cruz, "The Inclusion Imperative. Forging an Inclusive New Urban Agenda," The Journal of Public Space 2, no. 4 (2017): 1–20.

⁷ Pineda, V. S., & Corburn, J. (2020). Disability, urban health equity, and the promotion of inclusive urban development. The Lancet Public Health, 5(4), e197–e204. https://doi.org/10.1016/S2468-2667(19)30245-1

⁸ Between 2002 and 2007 I had the honor to help negotiate and then later implement this legally binding legal instrument in such diverse cities as Abu Dhabi to New Delhi. From Berkeley to Barcelona, to Belgrade, to Beirut.

abilities and older persons, have a seat at the table when funding and planning decisions are made. All too often, the needs of this community are overlooked in the development of strategies and policies.

I've seen firsthand the impact that exclusion and marginalization can have on a person's life. I spent the past 25 years as a researcher, practitioner, policymaker, investor, and social venture philanthropist advancing social justice and human rights around the world. There is tremendous value in raising up the voices and lived experiences of marginalized communities and ensuring that those voices include the perspectives of persons with disabilities and older persons. As such, this book also incorporates phenomenology and the lived experience of disability. In the context of disability rights and radical inclusion, phenomenology is a vital tool for understanding how individuals with disabilities experience and interact with the world, and how societal attitudes and structures may impact their ability to fully participate in society. By focusing on the subjective experiences of individuals with disabilities, phenomenological approaches like the ones I use at the beginning of each chapter center the reader on the societal attitudes and structures that limit or marginalize certain groups. This intentional approach makes visible the invisible challenges and efforts to promote greater inclusion by design.

For example, the phenomenological approach that opens each chapter might be used to study how others or I may experience or navigate the built environment, and how this experience is influenced by the design and accessibility of buildings and other physical infrastructure. This understanding has a proven track record of informing efforts to design more inclusive and accessible spaces that better meet the needs and capabilities of individuals like me who live with disabilities. By ignoring the subjective experiences of marginalized communities, including persons with disabilities, scholars risk perpetuating a deficit model that fails to value the unique knowledge and untapped human capital such communities hold. Failing to elevate phenomenology contributes to a lack of empathy and understanding among readers and potentially hinder efforts to promote greater inclusion and equality for the populations our readers are seeking to serve.

Overall, I see phenomenology as an indispensable tool for promoting greater understanding and empathy for the topics addressed in each chapter. Each chapter highlights not only emerging themes related to radical inclusion, but also allows readers to imagine the lived experience and what's at stake if we fail to get it right. By elevating the lived experiences of individuals with disabilities alongside other marginalized populations, we are informing efforts to promote greater equality and inclusion for all.

As you read through each chapter of the book, consider how you or your organization has addressed or perhaps failed to address the concept of inclusion in your policies, programs, and designs. And assess how your organization or profession responds to calls for more transparency, accountability, and participation from an increasing number of interconnected stakeholders.

Each chapter provides a clear overview of the concepts and practices that shape inclusion and discussion of the evolving notion of why radical inclusion is central to the future of cities. Each chapter aims to provide actionable and contemporary insights into the emergence of new factors that are affecting our communities and shaping the contours of our collective urban future.

In Chap. 1, I explore the core theme, radical inclusion, and argue that it is indispensable and too often overlooked. My approach to radical inclusion comes from the Greek word *radicalis*, which means getting to the root of the issue. So radical inclusion is not a militant or extreme position but rather an inquiry into addressing the roots of a new social contract. Radical inclusion, in this sense, is at the core of a new approach to social and economic development. What I am trying to show is that the idea of excluding people should in fact be viewed as the radical idea. That is, it leads directly to extreme harm, extreme neglect, and extreme moral deprivation.

In Chap. 2, as a counterpoint to the opening chapter, we explore the normative, ableist notions of othering, segregating, and marginalization. From explicit laws that punished persons with disabilities to implicit grand designs that planned for but planned out substantive and integrated approaches to full participation. This chapter also explores the new rising notions of modernity and urbanization.

Chapter 3 presents a constructive new approach to building the cities of tomorrow. This approach is radical inclusion. Here we revisit existing norms, theories, and social and spatial justice concepts. These approaches lead us toward a more nuanced approach to building inclusion, access, and belonging by design.

In Chap. 4, "How Cities Shape Our Experience," I offer a counterargument to reframe the question of feasibility by asking, what is the cost of exclusion? I offer insights into how to make these imaginary concepts material by detailing new approaches to constructing more inclusive and accessible spaces for all. Can these approaches lead us to a new normal, or perhaps are these approaches already the new normal? What will it take to put this new normal into practice?

Chapter 5 helps us answer the question, "How do we make and measure progress in radically inclusive cities?" I present a rapid assessment framework called the DisCo Policy Framework and offer the Iceberg of Inequality as a set of tools that can be used to benchmark progress effectively. This chapter contains insights that tie together a more integrated approach to understanding, measuring, monitoring, and governing a more inclusive, equitable, and accessible approach to urban development.

Chapter 6 looks toward the future and explores how emerging approaches and technologies will converge to unlock new capabilities for urban policies, plans, and designs. The future is accelerating, and we cannot predict how the convergence of AI, the metaverse, blockchain, drones, robots, and self-driving cars will affect our lives.

Chapter 7 explores the implications of "The Era of the New Normal." This chapter is a call to action and vigilance to ensure that we avoid repeating the same mistakes of the past and instead direct our attention toward a radically inclusive approach to unlocking human potential and building the future we need.

Now is the time for cities to prioritize inclusion and belonging at every stage of development. Only by working together and adopting a holistic approach can we create truly sustainable and equitable communities for all. There's a lot of work to do, there's no better time to start than now.

Mexico City, Mexico   Victor Santiago Pineda
December 18, 2022

References

Ferrari, L., Berlingerio, M., Calabrese, F., & Reades, J. (2014). Improving the accessibility of urban transportation networks for people with disabilities. *Transportation Research Part C: Emerging Technologies, 45,* 27–40.

Froehlich, J. E., Eisenberg, Y., Hosseini, M., Miranda, F., Adams, M., Caspi, A., Dieterich, H., Feldner, H., Gonzalez, A., & De Gyves, C. (2022). The Future of Urban Accessibility for People with Disabilities: Data Collection, Analytics, Policy, and Tools. *Proceedings of the 24th International ACM SIGACCESS Conference on Computers and Accessibility,* 1–8.

Guzman, L. A., Oviedo, D., & Rivera, C. (2017). Assessing equity in transport accessibility to work and study: The Bogotá region. *Journal of Transport Geography, 58,* 236–246.

Kempin Reuter, T. (2019). Human rights and the city: Including marginalized communities in urban development and smart cities. *Journal of Human Rights*, *18*(4), 382–402.

Libertun de Duren, N., Salazar, J. P., Duryea, S., Mastellaro, C., Freeman, L., Pedraza, L., Rodriguez Porcel, M., Sandoval, D., Aguerre, J. A., & Angius, C. (2021). *Cities as spaces for opportunities for all: building public spaces for people with disabilities, children and elders.*

Mercille, J. (2021). Inclusive smart cities: beyond voluntary corporate data sharing. *Sustainability*, *13*(15), 8135.

Pineda, V. S. (2020). *Building the inclusive city: governance, access, and the urban transformation of Dubai*. Springer Nature.

Pineda, V. S. (2008). Enabling justice: Spatializing disability in the built environment. *Critical Planning Journal*, *15*, 111–123.

Pineda, V. S., & Corburn, J. (2020). Disability, urban health equity, and the coronavirus pandemic: promoting cities for all. *Journal of Urban Health*, *97*, 336–341.

Pineda, V. S., Meyer, S., & Cruz, J. P. (2017). The inclusion imperative. Forging an inclusive new urban agenda. *The Journal of Public Space*, *2*(4), 1–20.

Rico, I. V. (2021). Smart cities for all: usability and disability bias. *European Review of Digital Administration and Law*, *2*(1), 157.

Acknowledgements

In the journey of bringing "Inclusion and Belonging in Cities of Tomorrow: Governance and Access by Design" to life, I have been fortunate to be surrounded by a constellation of brilliant minds and warm hearts. This book is not just a reflection of my thoughts and research but also a tapestry woven from the contributions of many who have influenced and shaped its course. First and foremost, I extend my profound gratitude to Dr. Serida Catalano, whose role as my closest collaborator and intellectual partner has been pivotal. Serida, your insights, unwavering support, and shared vision have been instrumental in shaping the narratives and ideas that form the backbone of this book. To my trusted colleagues, Dr. Sandra Willis and Milenko Podunavac, your expertise and perspectives have added invaluable layers to our discussions and debates, enriching the content of this book beyond measure. No words can adequately express my indebtedness to my mother, Dr. Maria Dubravka Pineda. Mom, you are my colleague, my inspiration, and, above all, my greatest teacher. Your life's work and ethos have been a guiding star in my professional journey, illuminating the path I've tread. My father, Ambassador Julio Cesar Pineda. Papa, your life's lessons have been a constant source of wisdom and the passion to build bridges. My grandmother, Nada Purkarevic, whose belief in me never wavered; my brothers and mentors Francisco Xavier Pineda and Patrick Atanasije Pineda, for challenging and helping me grow; my other brothers and champions Prof. Anand Vaidya, Zachary Kerschberg, Gallagher Fenwick, Jasko Begovic, Dr. Larry Lopez GSD, Luis Gonzalez, Gregorio Mendez—your encouragement and belief in me and my impact have been a source of continual motivation. Lastly, thank you to TH for our soulful union and our journey to awe and discovery. The wonder and beauty of life that we explore together have infused this book with joy and an essence that transcends the written word. This book is a tribute to all of you and to future scholars. Your collective wisdom, support, and love have not just shaped this work but also the person I have become. Thank you from the bottom of my heart.

Contents

1 Radical Inclusion: The Key to Urban Transformation 1
  Disability and Inclusive Development 2
  Transformation by Unlocking Capabilities and Removing Barriers 4
  Transformation by Overcoming the "Mismatch" 7
  What Is Universal Design? 8
  Can We Universally Design an Entire City? 12
  Climate Change Adaptation and Action 13
  Green and Blue Spaces and Corridors 15
  Questions to Guide Our Practice 19
  Callout Box—News Article 20
  References 20

2 The Legacy of Radical Exclusion in Cities 23
  Explicit Exclusion in Ugly Laws 27
  Implicit Exclusion in The Garden City 28
  The Faces of Oppression by Iris Marion Young 29
  If We Don't Intentionally Include We Unintentionally Exclude 31
    Planning for Neurodiverse and Autism Friendly Cities 31
    Urban Planning for Mental Health 33
  Callout Box—News Article 36
  References 36

xviii CONTENTS

3	**Constructing a New Approach to Radical Inclusion**	39
	The Need for Social and Spatial Justice	41
	Implicit Bias	44
	Justice as Fairness	46
	What Is Radical Inclusion?	48
	Disability Justice as a Lens for Advancing Radical Inclusion	49
	Defining Radical Inclusion as a Framework for Urban Transformation	51
	How Equity Relates to Justice	53
	Targeted Universalism as a Policy Tool for Radical Inclusion	53
	The New Reality	54
	Emerging Approaches to Radical Inclusion in Practice	55
	Callout Box—News Article	56
	References	57
4	**How Cities Shape Our Experience**	61
	The Cost of Exclusion and the Power of Imaginary Cities	63
	Making Imaginary Cities Real	66
	The Influence and Shortcomings of the Construction Industry	67
	Asset Management and Participatory Planning	68
	How the Pandemic Highlighted the Need for Integrated Approaches	70
	Challenges and Opportunities in Building Belonging by Design	73
	What Is the New Normal?	76
	Putting the New Normal into Practice	80
	Callout Box—News Article	81
	References	82
5	**Making and Measuring Progress in Radically Inclusive Cities**	85
	The DisCo Policy Framework	88
	Pillar 1: Legislative Measures (Laws and Norms)	88
	Pillar 2: Executive and Budgetary Support	90
	Pillar 3: Administrative and Coordinating Capacity	91
	Pillar 4: Participation of the Targeted Group	91
	Pillar 5: Attitudes Toward the Targeted Group	92
	The Iceberg of Inequality	94

Age-Friendly Cities	96
Age-Accessible Transportation	97
The Impact and Legacy of a New Urban Agenda	97
Radically Inclusive Cities in Practice	101
Adopt Standards to Advance Universal Accessibility in the Built Environment	101
Adopt Standards to Advance Accessibility Through Integrated, Multimodal Transportation Systems	102
Adopt Standards to Integrate Land Use, Climate Resilience, Historic Preservation With Social Inclusion	103
Case Study From the United Arab Emirates	104
What Can We Learn from This Case Study?	106
Callout Box—News Article	107
References	108

6 Emerging Trends in Cities of Tomorrow — 111

Cities of Tomorrow — 113
   Values, Priorities, and Targeted Universalism — 114
   How Do We Make These Values Real? — 117
The Fourth Industrial Revolution — 118
   Technology-Driven Transformation — 121
   Agile Cities and Buildings — 122
   Engineering New Approaches Through Partnerships — 125
   Data-Driven Urban Planning and Governance — 127
Callout Box—News Article — 130
References — 131

7 The Era of the New Normal — 133

Emerging Trends Accelerating the Speed of Urban Transformation — 136
Smart Cities Are Accessible Cities — 137
   What Can We Learn From These Cities? — 143
Emerging Trends Linking Radical Inclusion to Resilience in Practice — 144
   Pop Up Box: How Can We Finance Inclusive Urban Transformation? — 147

Where Do We Go From Here? 148
   Cities Are Not Waiting on the Sidelines, They Are Leading
     the Charge for Radical Inclusion 149
References 152

References 153

Index 161

List of Figures

Fig. 3.1	Four micro mobility solutions featured in black and white, over a green aqua background. These are being piloted and deployed in various cities. Few micro mobility solutions or options are designed for people with disabilities and older persons. (Source: Victor Pineda)	43
Fig. 4.1	Stevenson Square, Manchester, UK. Visual description: Diners eating at picnic tables placed in the street during the temporary "pedestrianization" of Stevenson Square to allow for more social distancing during the COVID-19 pandemic. (Source: David Dixon, April 13, 2021)	77
Fig. 4.2	St. Mark's Place, New York City. Visual description: Outdoor diners enjoy their meals in temporary shelters designed to allow restaurant-goers to eat outside while sheltered from the elements. These structures occupy part of the roadway, demonstrating how cities can reimagine street design for pedestrians. (Image credit: Eden, Janine and Jim, https://commons.wikimedia.org/wiki/File:Dining_on_St._Marks_Place_(50295553313).jpg)	78
Fig. 5.1	The Pineda Iceberg of Inequality. This diagram shows an "iceberg" or triangle where the first layer (under the water) lists basic freedoms: Access, Independent Living, Political and Public Participation, Mobility, and Awareness Raising. The second layer, above the water, is Basic Functioning and shows Education, Social Protection and Safety Nets, Employment, and at the top: Health, Habilitation, Rehabilitation	95

Fig. 7.1 Mockup of the Line plan. This image shows a mirrored building that is long and tall but very narrow. The mirrored surface reflects the desert and water from the ocean. (Image credit: NEOM, (2022) *NEOM. Accessed November 30, 2022.* (https://www.neom.com/en-us/regions/theline)) 142

Fig. 7.2 Design concepts for The Line project (NEOM, (2022) *NEOM. Accessed November 30, 2022.* (https://www.neom.com/en-us/regions/theline)). Digital mockup of the Line Project, this image shows abundant greenery with walking and swimming areas within an urban construction 143

CHAPTER 1

Radical Inclusion: The Key to Urban Transformation

Abstract Fifteen percent of the global population has a disability, which will only increase with aging demographic trends. The elderly population is expected to rise to 1.4 billion by 2030 and 2.1 billion by 2050. Half of the world's population already live in cities and cities will play an increasingly crucial role in promoting inclusion and addressing the needs of a rapidly changing demographic. As technology advances and assistive technologies are developed, disability will become increasingly common and cities must be transformed to be inclusive of everyone. The Capability Model argues that disability is not the attribute of the individual; instead, it is created by barriers that exist in the social environment and therefore requires social change. When barriers exist, inclusive communities work to transform the way they are organized to meet the needs of all people by mobilizing social, political, and economic factors to identify and eliminate participation barriers. Radical inclusion is a framework aimed at eliminating the barriers that hinder individuals and communities from reaching their full potential. It goes beyond full participation to create inclusive systems that promote equity and resilience. Inclusive communities aim to remove barriers that perpetuate poverty, inequality, disempowerment, isolation, and exclusion.

Keywords Radical inclusion • Disability • Agency • Equity • Resilience • Aging • Poverty • Capability deprivation

> *We all personally have, or know someone near and dear to us that has, some type of disability. That disability may be permanent or it may be temporary. Indeed each and every one of us will face all kinds of disabilities in our life. That is why it is so important that we design cities and our urban environments to meet the needs of all people.* (Alice Charles, Director for Integrated Cities, Planning and Design, ARUP)

As I arrived at Burning Man for the first time, I was struck by the vibrancy and creativity of the playa. Everywhere I looked, I saw people of all ages, backgrounds, and abilities coming together to create, explore, and celebrate. It was a world unlike any I had ever seen before, and I was immediately drawn to its energy and spirit.

As I began to learn more about the culture of Burning Man, I was introduced to the concept of radical inclusion. This concept, which is central to the Burning Man community, recognizes that everyone has something valuable to contribute, and that we are all stronger when we work together. It challenges the notion that some people are more worthy or deserving than others and instead celebrates the diversity and uniqueness of every individual.

This fateful day on the playa was a turning point in my academic journey. As I encountered the vibrant culture of Burning Man and learned about the concept of radical inclusion, I realized that this was an approach that could be applied to many of the issues I was studying in my field. I began to explore the ways in which radical inclusion could be used to address issues of social justice, equality, and empowerment, and I became determined to use my research to make a positive difference in the world.

In the years since my first encounter with radical inclusion at Burning Man, I have continued to be inspired by the spirit and values of the community. This book is a testament to the profound insights that have grown over time. In the following pages you will learn ways that you can incorporate a radically inclusive approach to your work, and I have done firsthand. The experiences and lessons I have learned at Burning Man, and I am committed to continuing to promote the values of radical inclusion in my research and teaching.

DISABILITY AND INCLUSIVE DEVELOPMENT

Radical inclusion is a framework that seeks to eliminate the barriers that prevent individuals and communities from exercising agency and achieving their full potential. It goes beyond promoting full participation and seeks to create inclusive systems that allow for greater equity and resilience.

Approximately 15 percent of people globally have a disability. And this proportion will only continue to rise due to aging demographic trends. More than half of all persons with disabilities[1] live in towns and cities. By 2030, this number is estimated to swell to between 750,000 and 1 billion.[2]

In 2017, the population over the age of 60 was already approaching 1 billion people, or 13 percent of the global population.[3] And of those, approximately 460 million older adults have one or more impairments.[4] This demonstrates the significant, self-evident, and interlined phenomenon, that is aging and disability. In 2030, the population over the age of 60 will rise to 1.4 billion or 17 percent of the projected global population, which will usher in a corresponding increase in the proportion of people who live with a disability. By 2050, it will be 2.1 billion or 21 percent of the population. Impairments will not be eliminated in the future, they will be multiplied, and since the launch of the United Nations Sustainable Development Goals and the COVID-19 pandemic, we are being called to accelerate what I call the inclusion imperative. We must build back better and co-design the world at scale to ensure that no one is left behind.

Persons with disabilities face dramatically higher poverty rates than the overall population. In some countries, poverty rates can be double that of persons without disabilities.[5] This has further consequential effects on people's health and their opportunities for education. Persons with disabilities also face digital barriers due to inaccessible websites or apps providing city services as well as barriers in the physical environment. In many cities, a lack of enforceable accessibility standards, lack of strict

---

[1] We will use persons with disabilities (as defined by the UN), as well as disabled persons. There is considerable debate with the disability community on the usage of person-first versus identity-first language to describe the experience and identity of disability. For the purposes of this book, I have chosen to alternate between person-first and identity-first language, using the terms disabled persons, disabled people, persons with disabilities, and people with disabilities. Under Article 1 of the UN Convention on the Rights of Persons with Disabilities (UNCRPD), persons with disabilities "include those who have long-term physical, mental, intellectual, or sensory impairments which in interaction with various barriers may hinder their full and effective participation in society on an equal basis with others." In addition, I want to recognize the scholarship and support of Dr. Catalano, who has accompanied me throughout the process of reviewing and completing this manuscript.

[2] WHO. (2011). World report on disability. World Health Organization, The World Bank.

[3] United Nations, Department of Economic and Social Affairs, "World Population Aging 2017 – Highlights," 2017, https://www.un.org/en/development/desa/population/publications/pdf/ageing/WPA2017_Highlights.pdf

[4] *Ibid*. WHO. (2011).

[5] United Nations. (2019). Disability and development report: Realizing the sustainable development goals by, for and with persons with disabilities. Department of Economic and Social Affairs. United Nations.

regulations, and lack of training, tools, and guiding documents impede progress. In addition, up to two trillion dollars is forgotten as lost income from excluding persons with disabilities from employment.[6]

As technology advances, people with disabilities will attain greater capabilities that improve their capacity to live productive lives. In Silicon Valley, the merging of biotech, medicine, IoT, cloud computing, and machine learning is unlocking unprecedented advances in assistive technologies. This means that more people with disabilities are leading more diverse, productive, and authentic lives.[7] There is a cultural shift occurring that is leading us toward fulfilling the promise of a better future for all. As more life-saving and life-extending technologies are developed, and as corresponding augmented and adapted human capabilities are unlocked by assistive technologies, we will see disability less as an oddity and more as the norm. Making cities age-friendly is an effective policy response to an aging population and ensures that physical and social environments exist that enable people to live healthy, independent, and autonomous lives into older age.

Transformation by Unlocking Capabilities and Removing Barriers

Nearly four billion people on earth already live in cities. And the population living in urban areas is increasing by 200,000 people per day. All of these new additions to urban environments need affordable housing as well as social, transportation, and utility infrastructure.[8] Cities shape virtually every aspect of global development, including the manner in which fundamental dignities and human rights are recognized, discussed, and implemented. This rapid urbanization has provided opportunities for transformational change, moving at an accelerated pace to improve social inclusion, access to services, and livelihoods. Cities also play a vital role in engaging marginalized populations that might otherwise be at risk of exclusion. How are we building our cities, and what rules and structures

---

[6] International Labour Office. (2009). The price of exclusion: the economic consequences of excluding people with disabilities from the world of work/Sebastian Buckup; International Labour Office, Employment Sector, Skills and Employability Department. – Geneva: ILO, 2009 85 p. (Employment working paper; no. 43).

[7] World Health Organization. N.d. Assistive technology. https://www.who.int/health-topics/assistive-technology#tab=tab_1

[8] Agenda, I., (2016), May. Shaping the future of construction a breakthrough in mindset and technology. In *World Economic Forum*.

are in place to ensure that they meet the needs of a rapidly changing demographic?

Inclusion is not about inserting persons with disabilities into existing structures, but about transforming systems to be inclusive of everyone. Amartya Sen[9] proposed the Capability Model, which was further developed by Martha Nussbaum[10] in the Frontiers of Justice.[11] I argue that their work helped advance my understanding of inclusion and provided a rich framework for my professional and academic journey to build cities of inclusion and belonging. The Capability Model focuses on the type of life a person is able to live, with "capability" defined as "practical opportunity." Under the Capability Model, disability is when an individual is denied or prevented from achieving practical opportunities as a result of their impairment. Thus, an individual is disabled when they are unable to do the things they value as a result of the interactions between their impairment and the social, cultural, economic, and built environment around them.

In this model, an "impairment is a prerequisite to disability," but it is its interactions with other characteristics (e.g., gender, age, race, etc.), the environment, and the resources at the disposal of the individual that cause capability deprivation, that is disability.[12] Unchecked barriers perpetuate exclusion, isolation, disempowerment, poverty, and inequality. In this sense, the Capability Model overlaps with the Social/Rights model of disability that sees disability as a social construct.[13] To be sure, disability is not the attribute of the individual; instead it is created by the social environment and requires social change. When barriers exist, inclusive

---

[9] Amartya Sen is an Indian economist and philosopher who is best known for his work on the causes of famine, welfare economics, and the capabilities approach to development and social justice. Sen has made many significant contributions to these fields, including his development of the concept of "capability deprivation" to describe the ways in which individuals are denied the opportunities to lead the kind of lives they value.

[10] Nussbaum's contributions to the capability approach and her critique of Rawl's theories of justice help us understand the ways in which individuals with disabilities are often denied or prevented from achieving their full potential due to the barriers and limitations they face.

[11] Nussbaum, M.C., (2007). Frontiers of Justice: Disability, Nationality, Species Membership, The Tanner Lectures on Human Values. Belknap Press, Cambridge, MA.

[12] Mitra, S., n.d. The Capability Approach and Disability 16. http://citeseerx.ist.psu.edu/viewdoc/download?doi=10.1.1.546.9171&rep=rep1&type=pdf

[13] We will introduce later Ed Soja's notion of Social and Spatial Justice to expand and tie together diverse and complementary theoretical approaches to building cities of inclusion and belonging.

communities work to transform the way they are organized to meet the needs of all people by mobilizing social, political, and economic factors to identify and eliminate participation barriers.

We often think of barriers on a smaller scale, such as the provision of wheelchair ramps or curb cuts. But in truth, many of these barriers exist at the macro level. This includes outdated laws and incoherent, incomplete, or outdated approaches to inclusion. These are intermingled with prevailing social attitudes that can include implicit bias, discrimination, prejudice, or general misconceptions about disability. These sometimes appear as fixed requirements and standards that create additional burdens, such as having affordable housing applications on an inaccessible website, or a medical or social welfare office housed in a public building with steps, or without proper signage or a working elevator.

Thinking about barriers in a systematic way encourages policymakers, designers, architects, engineers, construction companies, and service providers to confront very compelling and complex issues of contemporary societies in order to create capabilities. For example, spatial segregation, economic exclusion, lack of opportunities, and skills mismatches result in a majority of marginalized individuals in low-paying and sometimes informal jobs that don't provide them with any kind of reliable income. Lack of a formal address or identity may preclude access to formal jobs while lack of education and poor health can also restrict access to higher-paying jobs. Additionally, unaffordable transit fares and disconnection from the public transportation network further suppress access to economic opportunities. By acknowledging, identifying, and assessing barriers, pathways to bringing previously hidden issues to the surface are created. This in turn allows for collaborative designs and innovative solutions to be developed and implemented to make our cities and societies more inclusive and accessible for all.

The insights of Amartya Sen and Martha Nussbaum on the capability approach contributions on social and spatial justice can be applied to urban planning in several ways.[14] First, urban planners can use the capability approach to understand the ways in which the built environment and urban infrastructure can enable or disable the capabilities of individuals with disabilities. For example, planners can design accessible public transportation systems, buildings with ramps and elevators, and other features

[14] Amartya Sen applied this approach to issues of poverty, inequality, and social justice, arguing that these are not just economic problems, but also moral and political ones. Sen has received numerous awards and honors for his work, including the Nobel Memorial Prize in Economic Sciences in 1998.

that can help individuals with disabilities move around the city and access the same opportunities as those without disabilities.

Transformation by Overcoming the "Mismatch"

> For better or worse, the people who design the touchpoints of society determine who can participate and who's left out. Often unwittingly. A cycle of exclusion permeates our society. It hinders economic growth and undermines business success. It harms our collective and individual well-being. Design shapes our ability to access, participate in, and contribute to the world. (Kat Holmes, Author, Mismatch)

She sat down in my living room, leaned forward and said, "you don't know how excited I am to finally spend some time with you." It was 2014 and the brilliant and unassuming Microsoft executive named Kat Holmes was an inclusive design champion. Kat was just starting to formulate the core structure of her book, Mismatch. We shared stories of travels and mutual friends between sipping on afternoon tea. At some point, we started talking about human agency and she plunged into describing how mismatches have come to be a core litmus test for what would constitute effective or ineffective design. She described a mismatch happening between people and objects, either physical or digital, when the object doesn't fit a person's needs so that people then have to adapt themselves to make the object work. A wheelchair user, upon encountering a curb without a curb cut, is experiencing a mismatch. As is anyone who has ever tried to open a manual door with their hands full. Essentially, disability is the result of mismatched interactions under the social model of disability.

Mismatches make aspects of society accessible to some people, but not all people, which contributes to the societal invisibility of certain groups like people with disabilities. Radically inclusive cities identify, monitor, and respond to these mismatches, creating cities that work for all their inhabitants and in doing so, promote capabilities through the implementation of Universal Design principles. Every time we remedy a mismatched interaction, we are creating opportunities for more people to contribute to society in meaningful ways, which in turn increases the number of people who can participate in building the world that we want to create.[15]

I think my favorite example of technology that was introduced into the world without thinking clearly and including a broad set of perspectives is in public restrooms. The image I like to share is a toilet which has a sensor

---

[15] Holmes, K., (2006). *Mismatch: How inclusion shapes design.* MIT Press.

on the back of it for the flushing mechanism and it has a little sign on the wall that is not so intuitive and it tells you to wave your hand over the sensor in order to activate the toilet to flush. It's a great example of where I can just see somebody saying, "this is innovative, this is the future" but it's just such a perfect example of the kind of mismatches that happen when we pursue "innovation" without understanding who we've excluded in the process.

If you consider who might experience a mismatch in using that sensor, you realize that the whole system doesn't work for someone who is blind or has low vision and can't see the sensor or the sign. Or for someone who can't wave their hand or doesn't have a hand available. Or somebody who can't read English. As we put all those together we start to say, "wait a minute, who is this toilet designed for?" and it sends a signal of who is foreign and who isn't foreign or in essence, who's welcome and who's not welcome in that environment.

Without forethought, these mismatches occur over and over again. They occur anytime we introduce new technology into our cities such as payment touchpoints for transit systems or buying groceries. They generally occur when we remove a human from an environment and replace them with some kind of machine-based system. Each time we do this we create a new set of abilities that are required in order to be able to participate in that aspect of society. This is why I really love the questions "who might be excluded?", "who might experience a mismatch?", and "whose voice is missing from this process?" Because it is innate behavior to design to our own abilities and to our own preferences.

How do we build systems that identify and eliminate mismatches? How can we build belonging by design? Universal Design principles represent a highly effective starting point from which we can begin to unlock human capabilities and empower people to live the type of lives they have reason to value.

What Is Universal Design?

Accessibility is the bridge between a person's human rights and the fundamental freedoms that enable them to best make use of them. It helps to create an inclusive, productive, mobile, and peaceful society where people can engage with the built environment and one another. Our built environment strongly affects our quality of life as it is a determinant of where and how almost everyone lives, works, and plays. In the United

States for example, people on average spend nearly 90 percent of their time indoors.[16] So our access to those spaces and how they make us feel when we are in them is extremely important for our individual and collective wellbeing. But too often, a one-size-fits all approach is used to design buildings and urban spaces. For older persons or persons with a disability, this can mean navigating complex urban landscapes with many inaccessible public spaces.

The seven principles of Universal Design were developed to help guide the design of environments, products, and communications. The principles can be used to guide the design process, evaluate existing designs, and educate designers and citizens on the possibilities and features inherent in more usable products and environments. The goal of Universal Design is to maximize usability by individuals with a wide variety of characteristics. Some straightforward examples of effective Universal Design are things like curb cuts in sidewalks or the use of larger or color contrasting text in signage or other forms of public communications. Whether we are talking about learning strategies or physical space, Universal Design operates by a set of principles designed to maximize access to as many people as possible. The following examples were developed by the Center for Inclusive Design and Environmental Access at the University of Buffalo.[17]

Equitable use

The design is useful and marketable to people with a diverse range of abilities. For example, a counter space or desk surface may be raised or lowered to accommodate users of varying height, or to better suit an individual who uses a wheelchair.

---

[16] Shaping the Future of Construction: A Breakthrough in Mindset and Technology [WWW Document], n.d. *World Economic Forum*. URL https://www.weforum.org/reports/shaping-the-future-of-construction-a-breakthrough-in-mindset-and-technology/ (accessed 5.16.23).

[17] The Center for Inclusive Design and Environmental Access (IDeA Center) focuses on research, development, education, dissemination and design projects related to Universal Design. The IDeA Center is dedicated to enabling and empowering an increasingly diverse population by developing knowledge and tools that improve the human performance, health and wellness, and social participation of groups who have been marginalized by traditional design practices. The IDeA Center's activities are based on the philosophy of inclusive design, often called Universal Design or design for all.

Flexibility in use

The design accommodates a wide range of individual preferences and abilities. For example, a captioned video will allow people to choose to listen or to read in order to better understand content. This not only provides access to individuals with hearing impairments but also accommodates those who would rather not use sound or who naturally comprehend better through reading.

Simple and intuitive use

Use of the design is easy to understand, regardless of the user's experience, knowledge, language skills, or current concentration level. For example, a website that is well-organized with clear headings will facilitate access to information.

Perceptible information

The design communicates necessary information effectively to the user, regardless of ambient conditions or the user's sensory abilities. For example, a video includes a voiceover for individuals with visual impairments.

Tolerance for error

The design minimizes hazards and the adverse consequences of accidental or unintended actions. For example, a hallway is free of protruding objects at a height where they would not be detectable by someone with a visual impairment who uses a cane.

Low physical effort

The design can be used efficiently, comfortably and with a minimum of fatigue. For example, an automatic door opener can facilitate access to an office space or classroom.

Appropriate size and space for approach and use

Appropriate size and space are allotted for approach, reach, and manipulation regardless of physical characteristics such as size or mobility. For example, a classroom includes a range of seating options, including a table for someone who uses a wheelchair or wider chairs for individuals who are taller and/or larger.

Research from the International Labor Organization shows that the cost of excluding persons with disabilities equates to up to seven percent of national GDP.[18] It therefore makes complete sense for city leaders to invest in accessibility improvements in urban environments and services. When designed and built from the outset to follow Universal Design principles, additional costs of accessible urban infrastructure, facilities, and services are tiny, representing an increase of between zero and one percent. However, if these improvements are done as part of retrofitting or redesign exercises, then cities can expect significantly higher expenses.

A radically inclusive city understands and responds to mismatch and has the capabilities to promote, engage with, and implement principles of Universal Design at the city scale. To design a future for all, design must be used as a method for social change and must be incorporated from the very outset of infrastructure and urban development; in the planning stage. This initial phase needs to include input from all stakeholders, including those involved in the actual construction of projects as well as all stakeholders these developments are aimed at or affected by. Prominence needs to be given to project planning and scoping, for example by conducting sophisticated needs assessments and feasibility analyses.

This early phase should ideally incorporate the knowledge of all affected stakeholders as well as each of the companies involved in the construction in order to incorporate best practices at the most efficient cost basis. However, in practice the construction industry is one of the most fragmented in the world and is strongly shaped by the interplay between large numbers of participants along the supply chain and throughout the life cycle of projects and major urban developments, with the consequence that accessibility criteria are often poorly implemented, if not wholly neglected. Also, the companies tasked with building our cities rarely have the capacity to fully integrate accessibility into their established project management processes. For example many projects go to tender and even begin construction before detailed scoping has taken place. In addition, inclusive design practices and participatory planning principles are seen as luxuries and projects miss out on inclusive approaches to innovation and fail to utilize intangible resources or hidden cost saving measures.

To help address these challenges, governments, policymakers, and city leaders need to support the industry in enhancing its coordination and

---

[18] Buckup, S., (2009). The price of exclusion: The economic consequences of excluding people with disabilities from the world of work. *International Labour Organization*.

cooperative efforts along the entire extent of the value chain and jointly define and establish design and construction standards that lead to achieving common goals for the greater good.[19] Focusing on design also impacts other mechanisms including governance, creates better products and services, and encourages people to imagine structures that can solve problems at scale. Being intentional through design helps us build in radical inclusion instead of bolting it on. When cities are planned to follow the principles of Universal Design, everyone benefits.

CAN WE UNIVERSALLY DESIGN AN ENTIRE CITY?

In this chapter, we discussed the extent to which the "inclusion imperative" should be an inescapable priority for policymakers, designers, and service providers. Centering on inclusion is vital to not only realizing the sustainable development goals (and the broader 2030 Agenda), but also addressing a specific set of interconnected challenges that policymakers are confronted with such as inequality, an aging population, rapid urbanization, digital transformation, climate change, and migration flows, just to name a few.

Undoubtedly cities, towns, and municipalities are the locus of inclusive and accessible transformation not only because rapid urbanization makes it even more compelling to make cities places of belonging, but also in that the proximity between local governments and their dwellers can strongly contribute to co-creating new solutions, piloting new practices, and scaling successful approaches as new norms, which ultimately shapes more inclusive urban governance models.

Governments at the national level usually aggregate solutions for the greatest good. A senior policy maker at the US Federal Government confided, "National Governments tend to use a hammer instead of a scalpel." The obvious shortcoming here is that outliers are too often left behind. People that fall on the ends of the bell curve are simply forgotten. A radically inclusive approach at a local level would naturally be more nuanced. Local governments that center on inclusion also center their policies, programs, and initiatives on the "outliers," or people living on the margins. This means they design their policies using the basic premises of Universal Design, through a process of creating products that are accessible to

---

[19] See above: Shaping the Future of Construction: A Breakthrough in Mindset and Technology [WWW Document], n.d. *World Economic Forum*. URL

people with a wide range of abilities, disabilities, and other characteristics. In essence to benefit the greatest number of people without the need for specialized or separate designs.[20]

Building a municipal or urban governance model that empowers people to live the types of lives they value, that unlocks everyone's capabilities is not an ideal, it is not a dream. This is a necessity and a prerequisite to create scalable, robust, resilient, and antifragile[21] commodities or services that are provided without profit to all members of a society. Systems, agencies, or organizations that are antifragile benefit from shocks; they thrive and grow when exposed to volatility, randomness, disorder, and stressors and are enhanced by risk and uncertainty. Governments, private individuals, corporations, and civic organizations should approach risk and uncertainty as opportunities to identify and enhance failures or weaknesses in vital infrastructure, enhancing a system capable of serving us for the future we need.[22]

Climate Change Adaptation and Action

Globally significant problems such as climate change require new approaches to urban planning and design as well as transformative interventions. The necessity of these interventions is driven by a variety of existential challenges to existing infrastructure and involves new and more inclusive approaches to urban governance, policy, and design. Each of these approaches when applied to climate adaptation, net-zero carbon policy requirements, or broader sustainability initiatives must also consider radical inclusion as a cross cutting theme for shaping the future of cities:Climate change and its impacts can disproportionately affect marginalized communities so ensuring that climate adaptation policies and sustainability initiatives are inclusive is critical. The following are examples of how radical inclusion can be incorporated into governance and policy approaches to strengthen core outcomes:

---

[20] Universal Design means planning to build physical, learning, and work environments so that they are usable by a wide range of people, regardless of age, size, or disability status. While Universal Design promotes access for individuals with disabilities, it also benefits others.

[21] Anti-fragility goes beyond robustness; it means that something does not merely withstand a shock but actually improves because of it. The concept was developed by professor, former trader, and hedge fund manager Nassim Nicholas Taleb.

[22] A classic example of something antifragile is Hydra, the Greek mythological creature that has numerous heads. When one is cut off, two grow back in its place.

Building coalitions: In building coalitions to support climate adaptation and sustainability policies, it is essential to ensure that the voices and perspectives of marginalized communities are heard and included. This should involve engaging with disability rights advocates, community organizations, and other stakeholders to ensure that policies are designed to meet the needs of all members of the community.

Educating the public and conducting outreach: Educating the public and reaching out to communities that may be impacted by climate change and sustainability policies can help to build support and ensure that the policies are designed to meet the needs of those who may be most affected. This can involve providing information through public campaigns, public forums, and social media, as well as engaging with community leaders, hosting public forums, and conducting surveys to gather feedback from community members.

Developing partnerships: Developing partnerships with businesses, non-profit organizations, and other stakeholders can help to leverage resources and build support for policy initiatives that promote sustainability and radical inclusion. This can involve partnering with organizations that serve marginalized communities, such as disability rights organizations or organizations that work with low-income populations.

Providing data: Providing data on the experiences of marginalized communities, the costs and benefits of policies and the impact of policies on different stakeholders can help to build support for policy initiatives that promote radical inclusion. This can involve collecting and analyzing data on the impacts of climate change on different communities and sharing that data with policymakers and the public.

Engaging with the legal system: Engaging with the legal system to ensure that climate adaptation and sustainability policies promoting inclusion and accessibility are legally sound and can withstand legal challenges is also important. This can involve working with legal experts to develop policies that are legally defensible and engaging with the legal system to defend those policies when they are challenged.

Fostering a culture of inclusion: Finally, fostering a culture of inclusion within city government and among the public can help to build support for policies promoting inclusion and accessibility. This can involve training city staff on inclusive practices and values, as well as promoting a message of inclusion and accessibility through public outreach campaigns.

Green and Blue Spaces and Corridors

Green and blue spaces and waterways are becoming increasingly popular in urban planning as a way to address the challenges of climate change and promote sustainability. They also have additional benefits for the health and wellbeing of a city's residents, as these spaces have a proven positive impact on mental health. They are particularly important spaces for persons with disabilities, older persons, and people who are neurodiverse, as these people may be prevented from accessing some other recreational or natural environments due to preferences against visiting crowded or difficult to access locations. Green corridors are linear parks or strips of green space that connect different parts of the city, while blue corridors incorporate water features such as rivers and streams.

In addition to providing environmental benefits such as reducing the urban heat island effect and mitigating stormwater runoff, green and blue corridors also have significant social benefits. For example, bioswales[23] and rain gardens, which are commonly used in green corridors to manage stormwater runoff, can provide opportunities for gardening and urban agriculture, creating a sense of community ownership and pride. In addition, these green spaces can provide much-needed recreational opportunities, particularly for people living in densely populated areas with limited access to parks and gardens.

Green and blue corridors can also play an important role in promoting mental health and wellbeing. Exposure to nature has been shown to have positive effects on mental health, including reducing stress and anxiety and improving mood. For older persons and persons with disabilities, green and blue corridors can provide accessible and safe spaces for physical activity and social engagement, helping to combat social isolation and promote a sense of belonging in the community.

An example of a green corridor is The Promenade Plantée, which is a 4.7 km-long elevated park built on a former railway viaduct in the 12th arrondissement of Paris. It was one of the world's first green corridors and

---

[23] Bioswales are shallow, vegetated channels that capture and filter stormwater before it enters the sewer system. Rain gardens are landscaped areas designed to capture and absorb rainwater runoff from roofs, sidewalks, and other impervious surfaces. An example of a bioswale is the Westwood Rain Garden in Portland, Oregon, which is a community-led project that captures and treats stormwater from adjacent streets. An example of a rain garden is the Rain Garden Park in Olympia, Washington, which features several rain gardens that capture and filter runoff from a nearby park.

has inspired many similar projects around the globe. The park has become known for its beautiful gardens, scenic views, and the diverse wildlife that it attracts. Another example is the High Line in New York City. The High Line is a 2 km-long elevated park built on a former railway line in Manhattan. The High Line provides an attractive green space in the middle of a dense urban environment while also providing a unique perspective of the city.

The High Line, New York City Before and After

Image of the highline rail tracks before the area was renovated into public park space. Image shows two people walking along the tracks elevated above the city, which have become overgrown with weeds and grass. (Image credit: Dan Nguyen https://commons.wikimedia.org/wiki/File:Walking_tour_of_rail_yards,_before_it_became_the_third_and_final_section_of_the_High_Line.jpg)

1 RADICAL INCLUSION: THE KEY TO URBAN TRANSFORMATION 17

Image shows the renovated highline tracks, which are now a public recreation area. The image shows a crowd of people walking along the High Line, and in the background there are older brick buildings next to newer, larger, glass and metal buildings. (Image credit: Dan Nguyen https://commons.wikimedia.org/wiki/File:AHigh_Line_Park,_Section_1a.jpg)

For blue corridors, an example is the Chicago Riverwalk, which transformed the city's industrial riverfront into a public space with walking paths, seating areas, and restaurants. Another example is the Cheonggyecheon Stream in Seoul, South Korea, which was transformed from a polluted waterway and elevated highway into a natural and cultural amenity with walking paths, bike paths, and green spaces.

Cheonggyecheon Stream in Seoul Before and After

Image shows the Cheonggyecheon highway before it was removed as part of the river restoration project. Image shows an elevated highway next to a ground-level highway, with many cars driving along it. (Image credit: Cheonggye Expressway in 1972, 대한민국역사박물관 (National Museum of Contemporary Korean History) https://commons.wikimedia.org/wiki/File:Chonggye_Expressway_1972-05-20.png)

1 RADICAL INCLUSION: THE KEY TO URBAN TRANSFORMATION

Image shows the Cheonggyecheon Stream, located where the highway had been. Alongside the stream are walking paths and grassy areas and the image shows many individuals walking and sitting alongside the river. To the river's left and right are small, two-lane roads. (Image Credit: Grayswoodsurrey https://commons.wikimedia.org/wiki/File:CheonggyecheonSeoul.jpg)

By incorporating green and blue corridors into urban planning, cities can create more inclusive and welcoming spaces that respond to the needs of diverse populations. By providing accessible, safe, and beautiful spaces for physical activity, recreation, and social interaction, these corridors can foster a sense of community belonging and promote social cohesion. This can have significant benefits for public health and wellbeing, as well as for the overall livability and resilience of cities.

QUESTIONS TO GUIDE OUR PRACTICE

How might we empower people with new innovative solutions to build more inclusive and accessible cities? If a city is a complex system of systems, then how might we foster innovation in governance by design? Could we possibly create a cost-effective process to scale new more integrated solutions across all these urban systems? And how can those systems promote equity, access, inclusivity, and belonging? How can they be used to prevent marginalization and further empower persons with disabilities and older persons? It's not easy but in the following chapters, we will see how we can begin to Universally Design an inclusive city.

In this book, we will try to answer these questions by keeping in mind that there is no one-size-fits all solution. Instead, we have to be intentional in seeing the multiple dimensions of exclusion and recognizing that each of those dimensions requires a different approach.

Nevertheless, before starting our journey, it is vital to dig deep into the concepts that form the basic framework for radical inclusion and the main theories and approaches related to it, which is what we will do in the next chapter.

Callout Box—News Article

District faces disability rights lawsuit over bike lane designs
Source: The Washington Post

Consider This A lawsuit filed by two disabled women accuses the District of Columbia of adopting protected bike lane designs that make it harder for them to find safe parking, and which violates the Americans With Disabilities Act. This lawsuit highlights the need for urban planners to increase collaboration with all stakeholders, in this case to specifically consider the needs of individuals with disabilities, in their designs. The lawsuit resulted in changes to the design of bike lanes in Washington, D.C. and could potentially set a precedent for other cities to consider more open collaborative processes that center accessibility in their public planning processes.

References

Beasley, V. B. (2020). The Trouble with Marching: Ableism, Visibility, and Exclusion of People with Disabilities. *Rhetoric Society Quarterly*, *50*(3), 166–174. https://doi.org/10.1080/02773945.2020.1752127

Buckup, S. (2009). *The price of exclusion: The economic consequences of excluding people with disabilities from the world of work*. International Labour Organization.

Holmes, K. (2018). *Mismatch: How inclusion shapes design*. MIT Press.

Mitra, S. (2006). The Capability Approach and Disability. *Journal of Disability Policy Studies 16*(4), 236–247.

Nussbaum, M. C. (2007). *Frontiers of Justice: Disability, Nationality, Species Membership.* Belknap Press.

Pineda, V. S. (2008). Enabling justice: Spatializing disability in the built environment. *Critical Planning Journal, 15,* 111–123.

United Nations. (2019). *Disability and Development Report. Realizing the Sustainable Development Goals by, for and with Persons with Disabilities 2018.* United Nations, Department of Economic and Social Affairs.

United Nations, Department of Economic and Social Affairs. (2017). *World Population Aging 2017 – Highlights.* https://www.un.org/en/development/desa/population/publications/pdf/ageing/WPA2017_Highlights.pdf

World Economic Forum. (2016). *Shaping the Future of Construction: A Breakthrough in Mindset and Technology.* Retrieved May 16, 2023, from https://www.weforum.org/reports/shaping-the-future-of-construction-a-breakthrough-in-mindset-and-technology/

World Health Organization. (2018, May 18). *Assistive Technology.* Assistive Technology. https://www.who.int/news-room/fact-sheets/detail/assistive-technology

World Health Organization & World Bank. (2011). *World Report on Disability* (No. 978-92-4-156418-2). https://www.who.int/publications/i/item/9789241564182

Open Access This chapter is licensed under the terms of the Creative Commons Attribution 4.0 International License (http://creativecommons.org/licenses/by/4.0/), which permits use, sharing, adaptation, distribution and reproduction in any medium or format, as long as you give appropriate credit to the original author(s) and the source, provide a link to the Creative Commons licence and indicate if changes were made.

The images or other third party material in this chapter are included in the chapter's Creative Commons licence, unless indicated otherwise in a credit line to the material. If material is not included in the chapter's Creative Commons licence and your intended use is not permitted by statutory regulation or exceeds the permitted use, you will need to obtain permission directly from the copyright holder.

CHAPTER 2

The Legacy of Radical Exclusion in Cities

Abstract The cities we live in today continue to be largely inaccessible, unaffordable, and restrictive, leading to the intentional and unintentional exclusion of marginalized groups. This is the result of decisions made by various entities that influence the design of cities and create a sense of either exclusion or belonging. The lack of accessibility in the built environment perpetuates inequity and marginalizes difference, such as the exclusion of people with disabilities in employment due to inaccessible workplaces. The notion of exclusion was entrenched by the "ugly laws" in the Progressive Era, where persons with disabilities were prevented from commodifying their disability and punished for begging in public. The laws also reinforced the eugenic logic of segregation through the institutionalization of disabled individuals. If we want to build inclusive and resilient cities, we must understand the historical context and beliefs that have shaped our urban landscapes. And we must address the ways in which beliefs and assumptions about personhood, citizenship, and rights have shaped and continue to shape our cities.

Keywords Urbanization • Inaccessibility • Marginalization • Urban planning • Segregation • Exclusion by design • Bias • Structural oppression

> We have a myth in this country that we're all here because of our own efforts, that we're self-made. We have a myth that if you're poor, if you're living in ghettos or segregated neighborhoods, it's because you haven't tried hard enough. This mythology ignores the extent to which federal, state, and local government has created the very ghettos that we live in, and that these were intentional creations. (Richard Rothstein,[1] *The Color of Law: A Forgotten History of How Our Government Segregated America*[2])

In 1982, when I was only four years old and about to start school, my family lived in Caracas, Venezuela. The city was set in a tropical vibrant valley and was full of life. But this bustling modern metropolis was not built for a child like me. As my mother attended school enrollment appointments, she was filled with rage at the way every school would respond to her petition to enroll a child who had difficulty walking without assistance. She was systematically turned away, I was denied my right to education time after time.

The schools we visited seemed to have no room for a child like me, a child that was weak and had difficulty walking. I was seen as a burden, I was seen as a liability to the school, not as an asset. I could see the pain and sadness in my mother's eyes, and although I did not understand, I felt the sting of discrimination myself.

As a young adult I came to see how race repositioned and complicated my own lived experience, as a disabled person of color I navigated worlds of stigma, discrimination, and exclusion by design. Rothstien (2017) argues that the social and physical positioning of Black, Indigenous, and People of Color (BIPOC) in the United States was *"the result of racially motivated policies that violate our constitutional rights."* He argues that many institutions over time violated the principles of equal justice under law and fundamentally undermined the principles of democracy.

---

[1] Richard Rothstein's book "The Color of Law" exposes the history of racial segregation in the US housing market, arguing that it was deliberately enforced by federal, state, and local governments, through a series of policies and practices. Rothstein highlights policies such as racial zoning laws, restrictive covenants, redlining, and the construction of public housing projects in already-segregated neighborhoods. These policies have had long-lasting and devastating consequences, contributing to the persistence of racial inequality and the racial wealth gap in the United States. "The Color of Law" has received numerous awards and renewed public discussion and interest in the history and ongoing effects of racial segregation in American cities.

[2] Rothstein, R., (2017). The color of law: A forgotten history of how our government segregated America. *Liveright Publishing.*

The parallel between discrimination based on race and discrimination based on disability is clear—our current systems are built to exclude those who do not conform to certain standards. By recognizing and addressing these forms of discrimination, we can work toward a more just and inclusive society.

This insight has shaped my life in many ways. As an immigrant and a first generation American, I now understand that my experiences were not unique to the United States. All over the globe, I witnessed systems built on the premise of a "standardized student," with standardized tests, that advanced standardized workers, and led a standardized life. To be "normal," to fit the mold. As a human rights expert and senior government advisor, I came to see how destructive the normative notions of modernity excluded people by design. Specifically excluded people like me that did not fit the norm.

The underlying concept of radical exclusion, which is pervasive in public policy, architecture, and urban planning, has led us to build a world of segregation and apartheid. Children and adults with disabilities like me are too often denied the same opportunities as their non-disabled peers and are relegated to separate, often inferior, educational, work, transportation systems, and environments. These environments have essentially been built to exclude by design.

Despite the challenges, my mother's courage afforded me opportunities others took for granted. She continued to search for a school that would accept me, and eventually we found one in another country, in the progressive state of California. Ms Dearing at Roy O. Anderson Elementary school provided me with the support and accommodations I needed to enter the first grade, to learn alongside my peers. This experience changed the course of my education and my life. I now can offer technical guidance with first-hand experiences of radical exclusion to undo the systems and barriers that limit our collective potential. I can point out the misters that deny rights and share common policy and design errors that frustrate our progress toward building the cities and the futures we need.

As an urban planner and educator, it is evident to me that cities are at the center of this struggle. Cities as human systems are rife with exclusion and attempts to define what a "normal" body is by shaping the built environment around a normative ideal. The consequences of these efforts have produced cities that are inaccessible, inefficient, and poorly prepared to meet demographic projections or future needs. This chapter explores how this came to be by highlighting the history of these efforts, from so-called "ugly laws," punishing people with disabilities for being in public, to Ebenezer Howard's Garden City, which imagined a utopian city that defined spaces that cared for people with disabilities in a manner that segregated them from public life. Ultimately, this chapter sets up the basis from which to imagine how a radically inclusive urban future could better minimize the harm and build belonging by design in cities of tomorrow.

There is nothing inevitable about the cities we live in today. That they continue to be largely inaccessible or continue to intentionally and unintentionally create barriers for marginalized groups. That they are segregated, unaffordable, and restrictive. This is not by chance, nor is it an inevitable product of urbanization. Instead, as this chapter describes, the cities we have created continue to create inclusion and exclusion by design. Cities exist this way because of decisions made by planners, community members, city leaders, politicians, and commercial interests that create a sense of othering and/or belonging by design.

The continued exclusion of many varied groups in our cities has not always been wholly intentional, but it has always been a product of the physical manifestations of our biases, beliefs, and assumptions about who lives in cities and how they deserve to access space. During an interview with an executive at a large technology company, we came across the topic of radical inclusion by design. He succinctly stated the obvious, "If we don't intentionally include, we unintentionally exclude." With this understanding, it becomes vital to reassess our priorities in cities. What are the dominant contemporary social and moral values? Where is the compass to guide our actions, thoughts, and beliefs? Do our institutions have the capacity to manage and distribute justice (as we will see later in this chapter when discussing the "politics of difference"). If we are to build cities that are radically inclusive and resilient, we must understand the ways in which both modern and antiquated beliefs about personhood, citizenship, and rights have created cities that fail to work for everyone.

Theorists such as Iris Marion Young and Amartya Sen and Martha Nussbaum[3] laid the critical groundwork for this discussion with arguments such as Young's that structural oppression is the fundamental source of

---

[3] According to the capability approach, individuals with disabilities should be able to access the same opportunities and resources as those without disabilities, in order to live the kind of life they value and have reason to value. In her seminal book "Frontiers of Justice," Martha Nussbaum put forth a systematic, extensive, and influential capability theory of justice to date. Nussbaum aims to provide a partial theory of justice (one that doesn't exhaust the requirements of justice) based on dignity, a list of fundamental capabilities, and a threshold. Future scholars can explore its implication on social and spatial justice and how to further elaborate its implementation in practice.

injustice. This injustice in the built environment is the result of procedures and practices that perpetuate inequity, from inaccessible public transport to redlining.[4] These processes, Young argues, marginalize difference and perpetuate the understanding that there is a normative way to exist in the world. Young, in Justice and the Politics of Difference, defines marginal people as those that "the system of labor cannot or will not use" (p. 53) who remain marginal not because of their inability to work but because of societal definitions of what constitutes capable and worthy. These beliefs shape our environment, locking people with disabilities out of employment due to inaccessible workplaces, inaccessible streets, inaccessible transport systems, and societal beliefs about the capacities of those with disabilities.

Moreover, this chapter builds off the work of scholars such as Robert Imrie and most notably Susan Schweik who further consider the way attitudes and beliefs about people with disabilities, the elderly, and other groups continue to shape our urban landscape.

Explicit Exclusion in Ugly Laws

According to Susan Schweik's seminal research the first known "ugly law" ordinance was created in San Francisco in 1867.[5] It formed part of larger laws against begging and prohibited "certain persons from appearing in streets and public places." The certain persons were those who were "diseased, maimed, mutilated, or in any way deformed" (p. 25). Ugly laws were also known as "unsightly beggar ordinance." Other cities including Portland, OR., Chicago, Denver, Omaha, Columbus, Lincoln, New Orleans, and Reno all passed similar laws, as well as the state of Pennsylvania. The last known arrest of an individual under an "ugly law" occurred in Omaha, NE. in 1974.

Police sometimes faced difficulty enforcing such laws. Schweik notes that a 1921 New York Times article described how "the chief impediment to a general elimination of public begging is the sympathy of the public" and further explained that crowds would gather and prevent the officer from making an arrest. In an effort to limit such public support, the Charity Organization Society pushed for New York to pass an "anti freak

---

[4] A discriminatory practice by which banks, insurance companies, etc., refuse or limit loans, mortgages, insurance, etc., within specific geographic areas, especially inner-city neighborhoods.
[5] Schweik, S. (2009). The Ugly Laws: Disability in Public. *NYU Press.*

bill" to manage the problem of vagrants whose "deformities are exposed to the public gaze simply to excite sympathy" (p. 100).

According to Schweik, ugly laws more broadly prevented persons with disabilities from commodifying their disability, such as in the form of "freak-shows." Disabled people who lost access, or never had access in the first place, to gainful employment due to their disability were prevented from finding other ways to make money (p. 107).

According to Schweik, "ugly laws both reinforced and were impelled by a eugenic logic of segregation." Ugly Laws often included stipulations that replaced the mandatory fine or jail time with time in an almshouse for those who were disabled. Almshouses, however, provided largely temporary arrangements for those in their care, creating a revolving door beginning with an arrest under an ugly law citation and ending with a person being released from an almshouse only to return again. Predictably, widespread institutionalization grew out of the culture of ugly laws and was seen as a method of eugenics throughout segregation whereby disabled individuals were prevented from having children through lifelong institutionalization (p. 118).

The Progressive Era saw "deformed" individuals as problems that "would have to be managed as much as architecture, street layout or drainage," according to Schweik (p. 120). The "City Beautiful" movement of this era imagined great, beautiful cities that reserved public spaces for "the sanitized and regulated social body" (p. 122). Ebenezer Howard's "Garden City" plan exemplified the Progressive era focus on beautiful and well-organized cities by imagining a city consisting of "radially planned" small towns each connected to each other through transportation systems but surrounded by gardens, parks, and natural land. Howard's plan placed the sick, disabled, and otherwise deformed or unappealing out of sight in asylums, so-called epileptic farms, and homes for the poor. Schweik describes how plans such as Howard's provided the opportunity to create "disability-free boulevards" and that ugly laws served as "one of the many mechanisms... [for] policing space in the city" (p. 148).

Implicit Exclusion in The Garden City

Unlike explicit laws preventing people with disabilities from accessing public spaces (i.e., ugly laws), Ebenezer Howard's "Garden City" plan sought to keep disabled people on the periphery, relegating them to a life separated from the non-disabled.

Howard's Garden City is considered by many to be a utopian ideal for suburban living. Howard imagined radial communities with sections demarcated for public parks, businesses, industry, and housing. Each city had a population limit of 32,000, at which point a new radial community would be developed nearby. He imagined a community of seven cities, one in the center and the other six arranged in a circle outside, each connected to each other by canals and railways. Between each city, he imagined farmland, forests, reservoirs, cemeteries, and homes and asylums for people with disabilities, the unhoused, and orphaned, and those addicted to alcohol. Howard felt that urbanization and industrialization were causing declines in health and happiness and that his Garden City plan would both promote health and care for those who remain unhealthy (e.g., those with disabilities).

Howard imagined disability as the opposite of health and wellbeing, and he planned insane asylums, "epileptic farms," "blind colleges," and "convalescent homes" located between the cities, amidst farmland and forests. Rob Imrie, in his book *Disability and the City: International Perspectives*, argues that Howard's construction of health was directly "counterposed" to disability and "disablement," and as a result, he relegated "epileptics," "inebriates," the "convalescent," and the "insane" to segregated areas away from cities (Imrie, p. 121). Howard described these areas as "various charitable and philanthropic institutions" and argued further that "it is but just and right that the more helpless brethren should be able to enjoy the benefits of an experience which is designed for humanity at large" (Howard, p. 20). Susan Schweik, in her book *Ugly Laws*, further argues that Howard's garden city promised "disability-free boulevards" (p. 73).

THE FACES OF OPPRESSION BY IRIS MARION YOUNG

The decision to keep people with disabilities out of public view, through institutionalization, ugly laws, and inaccessible design, has shaped our cultural understanding of who belongs in a city. Ed Roberts, quoted in the book *The Disability Rights Movement: From Charity to Confrontation*, described how legislators, when pushed on the need to build curb cuts, said "Curb cuts, why do you need curb cuts? We never see people with disabilities out on the streets. Who is going to use them?"[6] As stated by Prince (2008) "The history of urbanization for people with disabilities involves a history of institutional segregation, sterilization, charitable

---

[6] Fleischer, D. Z., & Zames, F. (2013). *The disability rights Movement: From charity to confrontation*. CNIB.

responses to needs, stigma, and prejudice, and the medicalization of conditions and identities."[7]

Iris Marion Young, in Justice and the Politics of Difference, argues that "justice should refer not only to distribution, but also to the institutional conditions necessary for the development and exercise of individual capacities and collective communication and cooperation" (p. 39). Young describes how marginalization expels a wide range of individuals and groups from "useful participation in social life" potentially condemning them to "severe material deprivation and even extermination."

The built environment has played a key role in reproducing the marginal status of people with disabilities. Radically inclusive cities value, defend, and promote difference in urban spaces. The normative built environment throughout the world only includes those groups deemed normative and otherwise socially acceptable. City blocks, inaccessible due to crumbling cement or lack of curb cuts, provide access to only those unencumbered by such barriers. Buildings, parks, community centers, and other markers of urban social life, that are unreachable by public transit or inaccessible due to design, define what is normative, acceptable, and otherwise valued in those spaces. Young argues that "by definition, a public space is a place accessible to everyone" and that "social justice in the city requires the realization of politics of difference" (p. 240). Social justice therefore demands targeted policies to ensure that all groups are included and can participate.

In the urban environment, realizing the politics of difference means building spaces that do not create barriers or prevent participation and rather promote and defend the access of all groups. A city that does not prioritize the access and inclusion of persons with disabilities has decided that disabled people do not have the same value or citizenship worth as those without disabilities. In other words, treating all people the same creates unequal results; cities that do not promote politics of difference choose instead to protect only what they view as normative. Requiring all people to climb stairs into the library is perhaps equal, but not equitable or inclusive.

Robert Imrie in Disability and the City argues that "the built environment has a physical inertia that resists change to the extent that many come to view city structures and spaces as almost fixed and immutable" (p. 11). He further asserts that the general public falsely assumes that the city is able to provide access for most people and thus those unable to

---

[7] Prince, M. J. (2008). Inclusive city life: Persons with disabilities and the politics of difference. *Disability Studies Quarterly, 28*(1).

access it in its current form are responsible for figuring out alternatives. Of course, even non-disabled people face barriers when interacting with the built environment, either because the design was inherently flawed or due to a city's failure to prioritize routine repairs or upgrades. Imrie argues, as I have earlier in this book, that cities embody the cultural and sociopolitical zeitgeist of their time. He points out that racial and socio-economic inequalities are literally "mapped" onto cities in the form of redlining, gentrification, and suburbanization.

Our socio-institutional beliefs against persons with disabilities are also mapped onto our cities. Imrie argues that a key contributor to the continued economic marginalization of persons with disabilities is the belief that "disabled people are characterized by poor and/or limited work abilities." As stated above, many dwellers remain marginal not because of their inability to work but because of societal definitions of what constitutes capable and worthy. These beliefs shape our built environment, locking people with disabilities out of employment due to inaccessible workplaces and public transportation systems.

IF WE DON'T INTENTIONALLY INCLUDE WE UNINTENTIONALLY EXCLUDE

Cities and urban settlements inherently wrestle with a spatial dimension of the social contract, specifically who belongs in the city, and who can be considered a citizen of that city. What is an ideal citizen and what values does the city uphold? Every city leader that I have worked with or interviewed to some degree either apologizes for or flatly rejects any possible shortcomings with respect to their work access, equity, or exclusion. Cities around the world make headlines with racial, economic, and ethnic tensions that occasionally manifest somewhere along the continuum of protest, civil unrest, or regime change.

Planning for Neurodiverse and Autism Friendly Cities

The concept of designing environments specifically for people with autism is relatively new. It has only been in the last few decades that the needs of people with autism have been widely recognized and addressed in the design of public spaces.

One of the earliest examples of autism friendly design can be traced back to the 1990s, when a group of parents in the United Kingdom created a sensory garden for their children with autism. This garden, which was specifically designed to be relaxing and not overstimulating, was one of the first examples of a public space that was tailored to the needs of people with autism.

Since then, the concept of autism friendly design has gained more mainstream attention and has been applied in a variety of settings, including schools, homes, and public buildings. Today, there are numerous organizations and experts around the world who are dedicated to promoting autism friendly design and providing resources and guidance to those interested in creating more inclusive environments for people with autism.[8]

There are a few key actions that can be done to make cities or spaces more autism friendly:

Establish guidelines and standards: Developing clear guidelines and standards for autism friendly design can help ensure that new buildings and public spaces are designed with the needs of people with autism in mind. These guidelines could be based on best practices from other countries and should be developed in consultation with experts and people with autism.

Provide sensory-friendly public spaces: Many people with autism have sensory processing issues, so it's important to create public spaces that are aimed at being calming rather than overstimulating environments. This might include quiet rooms or outdoor spaces with fewer visual and auditory distractions.

Make transportation accessible: People with autism may have difficulty navigating unfamiliar environments or using public transportation.

---

[8] This includes Debra Muzikar, the founder of the Autism Asperger's Digest magazine and the creator of the Autism Awareness Center website. She is an expert on designing sensory-friendly spaces for people with autism and her work along with the work of others in the field serve to highlight that sensory issues of autism are very real and can be very debilitating for individuals on the autism spectrum. Therefore designing for autism requires a thoughtful and empathetic approach that takes into account the unique sensory needs of individuals on the autism spectrum. Another expert in the field is Elizabeth C. Cushing, an architect and the founder of Cushing Terrell, an architecture and engineering firm that specializes in designing for people with autism and other special needs. She is working to address the fact that designing for people with autism requires a deep understanding of their unique needs and perspectives, as well as a commitment to creating spaces that promote inclusion and dignity. Important institutions in this area include The Center for Autism and the Built Environment (CABE). CABE is a research center at the University of California, Davis that focuses on designing environments that are supportive for people with autism. They have published numerous important research studies and guidelines on autism friendly design.

Ensuring public spaces are physically easily accessible and providing clear signage and wayfinding tools, as well as training staff to be aware of the needs of people with autism, can help make transportation more accessible.

Promote social inclusion: People with autism may struggle with social interactions, so it's important to create opportunities for them to participate in their community. This might include supporting groups and activities specifically for people with autism or providing training and support for businesses to be more inclusive of people with autism.

Provide information and resources: Providing information and resources about autism to the public can help raise awareness and understanding of the needs of people with autism, which can lead to more inclusive communities.

Pop out Box: Case Study on Autism Friendly Hotel
A quick practical application of guidelines and measures to make an accessible, autism friendly hotel may include:

1. Designing guest rooms with sensory-friendly features such as blackout curtains, white noise machines, and weighted blankets.
2. Providing social skills training for hotel staff to help them communicate effectively with guests with autism and manage behaviors as needed.
3. Offering a range of accessible room options, including wheelchair-accessible rooms and rooms with visual fire alarms for guests with hearing impairments.
4. Providing information and resources about the local area for guests with autism, including maps with clear wayfinding and lists of sensory-friendly activities and attractions.
5. Implementing technology such as assistive communication devices and sensory aids to support guests with autism during their stay.

Urban Planning for Mental Health

Design and urban planning interventions aimed at improving mental health may differ from those aimed at creating autism friendly cities in some ways, but there are also many similarities between the two approaches. One key similarity is the importance of creating environments that are sensory-friendly and comfortable for all users. This may involve designing public spaces that are quiet and calming, with minimal visual clutter and comfortable seating options. Both approaches may also incorporate the use of technology to create more accessible and inclusive environments. In the case of mental health, this may involve the use of virtual reality (VR) or augmented reality (AR) to create immersive environments that promote relaxation and stress reduction.

However, there is also the need to recognize the distinctions that are necessary between the different approaches. One key difference is that interventions aimed at improving mental health may need to address a broader range of mental health issues including depression, anxiety, and post-traumatic stress disorder (PTSD), among others. This may require a more comprehensive approach that includes not only physical design changes but also changes to policies, programs, and services.

In both cases, it is also important to involve people with lived experience in the design and planning process to ensure that their needs and perspectives are taken into account. This can help to promote more integrated approaches by ensuring that everyone, regardless of ability or mental health status, has a say in the design of the spaces and services that they use.

Examples of effective and specific design and policy interventions that can be implemented in cities to improve the impacts of depression, anxiety, and post-traumatic stress disorder (PTSD) include:

Green and blue spaces: Access to green or blue spaces[9] has been linked to lower levels of depression, anxiety, and PTSD. Cities can create more parks and green spaces or retrofit existing spaces to make them more inviting and accessible to everyone.[10] This can include adding more trees and plants, installing seating areas and providing amenities like water fountains and restrooms.

Active transportation: Encouraging active transportation, such as walking or cycling, can help to promote physical activity and reduce the risk of depression and anxiety. Cities can create more pedestrian and bicycle-friendly infrastructure such as bike lanes, pedestrian crossings, and safe routes to school. Additionally, providing amenities like bike-sharing

---

[9] Green spaces and waterways are popular in urban planning as a way to address the challenges of climate change and promote sustainability. See more in Chap. 1.

[10] Bergou, N et al. (2022). The Mental Health Benefits of Visiting Canals and Rivers: An Ecological Momentary Assessment Study. *Plos One 17, no. 8* e0271306.

programs with accessible trikes or three wheeled bikes and secure bike parking can make it easier for people to facilitate accessible journeys and choose active transportation.[11]

Sensory-friendly public spaces: Cities can create sensory-friendly public spaces and transportation systems (such as quiet carriages) that are designed to be calming and comfortable for all users. This was showcased in Doha during the city's hosting of the 2022 World Cup. The games were promoted as the most accessible global sporting event in history. Key features in the stadiums and other sporting infrastructure included rooms for reducing noise levels, minimizing visual clutter, and providing diverse seating options that are comfortable for people with different sensory needs.

Accessible mental health services: Cities can work to ensure that mental health services are accessible and affordable for all residents. This can include providing funding for mental health clinics and support groups, offering telehealth services for people who cannot physically visit a clinic, and ensuring that mental health services are covered by insurance.

Inclusive public engagement: Cities can engage with residents in an inclusive way to ensure their voices are heard in the planning and design process. This can include conducting community meetings in accessible locations, providing interpretation and translation services, and working with community-based organizations to reach a wider range of residents.

Overall, while there may be some differences between interventions aimed at creating autism friendly cities and those aimed at improving mental health, there are also many similarities. By taking a comprehensive and inclusive approach to design and planning, we can create urban environments that promote both physical and mental wellbeing for all users. New approaches are evolving throughout Europe to deploy more holistic solutions that also link mental health and wellbeing to culture, circular economy, and environmental protections through the reimagining and re-using open spaces and buildings.[12]

---

[11] Huang, X, White, M and Langenheim, N. (2022) Towards an Inclusive Walking Community—A Multi-Criteria Digital Evaluation Approach to Facilitate Accessible Journeys. *Buildings 12, no. 8 (2022): 1191.*

[12] Ricci, L (2022). Integrated Approaches to Ecosystem Services: Linking Culture, Circular Economy and Environment through the Re-Use of Open Spaces and Buildings in Europe. *Land 11, no. 8 (2022): 1161.*

In the next chapter I will present a constructive new approach, that of Radical Inclusion, to building cities that are better suited to realize a more just, fair, equitable, and barrier-free future.

Callout Box—News Article

Why accessible sidewalks fall by the wayside[13]
Source: Planetizen

Consider This Despite the passage of the Americans with Disabilities Act more than 30 years ago, many U.S. cities delay making accessibility improvements to sidewalks until activists bring them to court. Cities including Los Angeles, Baltimore, Long Beach, Calif. and Portland, Ore. have all been sued for dangerous sidewalk conditions, but even the suits that advocates win can take decades to translate into real results on the ground. Funding accessible and well-maintained networks of sidewalks should be a basic civil right, not something that occurs only once lawyers get involved, and would make a far greater difference to people with mobility challenges than winning lawsuits.

The fact that cities often delay making accessibility improvements to sidewalks until activists bring them to court demonstrates that the passage of legislation doesn't necessarily translate into compliance or lead to the outcomes the legislation was designed to enact. By dragging these cases through the courts, it means that there are extended periods of time where people with disabilities are exposed to dangerous or mobility-limiting conditions in the streets and spaces of their cities. It is time for cities to proactively fund and maintain accessible networks of sidewalks as a basic civil right.

References

Bergou, N., Hammoud, R., Smythe, M., Gibbons, J., Davidson, N., Tognin, S., Reeves, G., Shepherd, J., & Mechelli, A. (2022). The mental health benefits of visiting canals and rivers: An ecological momentary assessment study. *Plos One*, *17*(8), e0271306. https://doi.org/10.1371/journal.pone.0271306

---

[13] Ionescu, D (2022) Why Accessible Sidewalks Fall by the Wayside. *Planetizen*, November 15, 2022 https://www.planetizen.com/news/2022/11/119678-why-accessible-sidewalks-fall-wayside

Chan, Kok Hui, J. (2020, September 3). Rebuilding cities better in the post-COVID-19 world. *Asia Global Institute.* https://www.asiaglobalonline.hku.hk/rebuilding-cities-better-post-covid-19-world

Fleischer, D. Z., & Zames, F. (2011). *The Disability Rights Movement: From Charity to Confrontation.* Temple University Press. http://www.jstor.org/stable/j.ctt14bt7kv

Frey, W. (2021). Pandemic population changes across metro Americ: Accelerated migration, less immigration, fewer births and more deaths. *Brookings.* https://www.brookings.edu/research/pandemic-population-change-across-metro-america-accelerated-migration-less-immigration-fewer-births-and-more-deaths/

Graham, G., Ostrowski, M., & Sabina, A. (2015, August 6). Defeating the zip code health paradigm: Data, technology, and collaboration are key. *Health Affairs Blog.* https://www.healthaffairs.org/content/forefront/defeating-zip-code-health-paradigm-data-technology-and-collaboration-key

Harvey, D. (1973). *Social justice and the City.* The University of Georgia Press.

Huang, X., White, M., & Langenheim, N. (2022). Towards an Inclusive Walking Community—A Multi-Criteria Digital Evaluation Approach to Facilitate Accessible Journeys. *Buildings, 12*(8), 1191. https://doi.org/10.3390/buildings12081191

Ionescu, D. (2022, November 15). Why Accessible Sidewalks Fall by the Wayside. *Planetizen.* https://www.planetizen.com/news/2022/11/119678-why-accessible-sidewalks-fall-wayside

Lefebvre, H., Kofman, E., & Lebas, E. (1996). *Writings on Cities.* Blackwell Oxford.

Prince, M. J. (2008). Inclusive City Life: Persons with disabilities and the politics of difference. *Disability Studies Quarterly, 28*(1).

Ricci, L. (2022). Integrated Approaches to Ecosystem Services: Linking Culture, Circular Economy and Environment through the Re-Use of Open Spaces and Buildings in Europe. *Land, 11*(8), 1161.

Rothstein, R. (2017). *The Color of Law: A forgotten history of how our government segregated America.* Liveright Publishing.

Schweik, S. M. (2009). *The Ugly Laws.* New York University Press.

Singru, R. N. (2021, April 8). The digital transformation caused by the pandemic can be a powerful tool for inclusive city planning. *Asian Development Blog.* https://blogs.adb.org/blog/digital-transformation-caused-pandemic-can-be-powerful-tool-inclusive-city-planning

Soja, E. W. (2013). *Seeking Spatial Justice.* University of Minnesota Press.

University of California Television (UCTV). (2008, January 31). *Martha Nussbaum – Conversations with History.* https://www.youtube.com/watch?v=Qy3YTzYjut4

Open Access This chapter is licensed under the terms of the Creative Commons Attribution 4.0 International License (http://creativecommons.org/licenses/by/4.0/), which permits use, sharing, adaptation, distribution and reproduction in any medium or format, as long as you give appropriate credit to the original author(s) and the source, provide a link to the Creative Commons licence and indicate if changes were made.

The images or other third party material in this chapter are included in the chapter's Creative Commons licence, unless indicated otherwise in a credit line to the material. If material is not included in the chapter's Creative Commons licence and your intended use is not permitted by statutory regulation or exceeds the permitted use, you will need to obtain permission directly from the copyright holder.

CHAPTER 3

Constructing a New Approach to Radical Inclusion

Abstract Spatial justice is an approach to social justice that takes into account the organization and utilization of geographical space and its impact on human life and social relations. Geographical location plays a key role in producing spatial injustice and exacerbating disadvantages. The social is spatial and vice versa, which is critical to understanding the experiences of marginalized individuals and communities. Despite progress in legislation, planning practitioners have not fully realized the enabling power of physical space and dominant models of disability continue to remain unjust. The organization of space and urban planning are crucial to promoting spatial justice, as studies have shown that a person's ZIP code is a stronger predictor of health than any other factor. Public-private initiatives have often failed to consider the spatial dimension of justice in their designs and have neglected to address the exclusion of people with disabilities. The current social contract ignores the spatiality of injustice and a new social contract centered on space must be developed to reframe the problems and solutions to equity, access, and inclusion in human settlements.

Keywords Spatial justice • Urban transformation • Social justice • Geographical space • Implicit bias • Spatial dimension • Social contract • Equity

> *When I say accessible, I don't mean just for people with disabilities. Because when we work on the accessibility of public spaces, we also need to think about older persons. And the shopping carts and the strollers. And the mothers and fathers that take their children to school. It's about having the ambition to build a city that is kind to everyone. And when I say everyone, I mean everyone. Without any kind of exclusion.* (Joan Ramon Rivera, Advisor for Town Hall of Barcelona, President of the National Municipal Institute of People with Disabilities)

As I arrived at UC Berkeley on my first day of college, I was struck by the vibrant energy and diverse community that surrounded me. The campus was a melting pot of cultures, identities, and experiences, and I felt a sense of belonging and acceptance that I had never experienced before. I did not need to prove myself or fight twice as hard to be seen. I felt a sense of awe and reverence as I walked among the same hallowed halls as Martin Luther King, John F Kennedy, and role models who had come before me. These were also people like Judith Heumann[1] and Ed Roberts[2] who had paved the way for disability rights. I knew I would be part of a lineage of social change, of a new school of thought, and I felt a deep sense of gratitude and respect for the efforts of those that came before me.

As I explored the campus, I was awestruck by how accessible it was, the beauty and grandeur of the buildings and the towering redwood trees, the sweeping views of the Bay, the bustling streets and squares—it was all so alive, accessible, and full of possibility. I couldn't help but feel a sense of awe and reverence as I took it all in. But as I walked, I still noticed some ways in which the campus fell short when it came to inclusion and belonging. The foundations of today's urban questions are social and spatial justice, and I couldn't help but wonder what it really meant for all people to feel included, rather than just be included on paper. I wondered what happens when inclusion efforts fail, or when municipal policies, programs, or services exclude segments of the population explicitly or implicitly.

---

[1] Judith Heumann: Heumann is a disability rights activist and a leading advocate for the rights of people with disabilities. She has worked to improve accessibility and inclusion for people with disabilities in education, employment, and other areas of life. Also a Berkeley Alum, her life is featured in the documentary films Crip Camp (Higher Ground and Netflix) and Lives Worth Living (PBS).

[2] Ed Roberts: Roberts was a disability rights activist and the first severely disabled student to attend the University of California, Berkeley. He is credited with helping to establish the independent living movement, which seeks to enable people with disabilities to live as independently as possible.

I knew that my time at UC Berkeley would be a chance to explore these questions, to learn and grow, and to make a difference in the world. And as I settled into my new life on campus, I felt a sense of purpose and determination to do just that. Whether through my studies, my activism, or my daily interactions with my peers, I knew that I had the power to contribute to a more inclusive, just, and equitable society. I was filled with a sense of belonging and hope for the future. I hoped that I could help to shape and build the more inclusive and accessible future that I had imagined and knew needed to be created.

In order to understand how we can truly make cities become places of belonging for all, we first need to explore not only what it really means for all people to be included but rather to feel like they belong. Likewise, we must understand what happens when inclusion efforts fail, or when municipal policies, programs, or services exclude segments of the population explicitly or implicitly. The foundations of today's urban question continue to be social and spatial justice. However, the precipice for urban transformation is not social or spatial justice, but rather pandemics, climate change, social cohesion, immigration flows, and an emerging transformation of the future of work, just to name a few. Each of these factors and forces require us to reimagine human dignity through a new social contract, one that must inherently also be spatial.

This chapter outlines the theoretical gaps in inclusive theories that have impeded true inclusion efforts, before considering what a new approach to radical inclusion would provide for cities and all the systems within them. It also further explores the role of disability justice theories as a lens for advancing radical inclusion.

The Need for Social and Spatial Justice

The term "spatial justice" was developed by radical geographers such as Lefebvre,[3] Soja,[4] and Harvey[5] (Soja 2013; Lefebvre 1996; Harvey 1973). Each approaches the ideas of social justice with the organization and utilization of geographical space. To be sure, spatial justice theorists contend that space is an active force that impacts and deeply shapes human life and

---

[3] Lefebvre, H. (1996). The Right to the City. In: Kofman, E. and Lebas, E., eds. *Writing on Cities*. Oxford: Blackwell Publishers.

[4] Soja, E. W. (2013). Seeking Spatial Justice. *Minneapolis: University of Minnesota Press*.

[5] Harvey, D. (1973). Social Justice and the City. *Athens: University of Georgia Press*.

all ranges of human activities and social relations. Therefore, there is an inextricable relation between human beings and space, in that not only the space determines the social, but the social in turn builds the space, by constructing and reinforcing conceptions and norms of the space itself. It follows that social justice in order to be realized also requires the spatial dimension of justice to be taken into consideration. Spatial justice ultimately compels us to deal with the repercussions, in terms of burdens and benefits, that urban development entails.

Most notable are works of two friends and former teachers, the geographers David Harvey and Edward W. Soja who helped me understand and position human agency in a geographical frame. While listening to Edward W. Soja, I came to understand that spatial justice seeks to promote more progressive and participatory forms of democratic politics and social activism and provides new ideas on how to mobilize and maintain cohesive coalitions and regional confederations of grassroots and justice-oriented social movements. I came to understand that spatial justice is "a struggle over geography."[6]

The organization of space is of fundamental importance to contemporary urban planning as studies show that a person's ZIP code is a stronger predictor of his or her overall health[7] than any other category or distinction including, race, gender, and age. Geographical location therefore appears to be a key element in producing spatial injustice, exacerbating disadvantages while also reinforcing privileges. I have witnessed this through my travels from Cuba to Yemen, Varanasi to Berkeley.

As stated above, the spatial is the social and it reflects and makes material social norms in a very physical and tangible manner. Think of bike shares and other micro mobility vehicles;[8,9] these services conceptualize micro mobility for a standard persona with capabilities that rarely deviate from an ideal, thus resulting in tools that further exacerbate the exclusion

---

[6] *Ibid.* Soja, E.W., (2013). *Seeking spatial justice* (Vol. 16).

[7] Graham, G., Ostrowski, M. and Sabina, A., (2015). Defeating the zip code health paradigm: data, technology, and collaboration are key. *Health Affairs Blog, 6.*

[8] Micro mobility devices include bicycles, e-bikes, electric scooters, electric skateboards, shared bicycles, and electric pedal assisted (pedelec) bicycles.

[9] NACTO recently released the latest point-in-time look at ridership numbers across this still fast-changing mode of transportation. We found that from 2010–2016 there were 88 million trips taken on bike-share systems across the United States. Since then, growth skyrocketed: in 2019 alone, people took 136 million trips. All told, over the past decade, a third of a billion trips were taken on shared bikes and scooters.

Fig. 3.1 Four micro mobility solutions featured in black and white, over a green aqua background. These are being piloted and deployed in various cities. Few micro mobility solutions or options are designed for people with disabilities and older persons. (Source: Victor Pineda)

of people with disabilities and their ability to use the space on an equal basis with others.

In essence, the great majority of these public-private initiatives have done little to think through radical inclusion in the design or deployment of these services and have neglected the spatial dimension of justice (Fig. 3.1).

Despite progress in legislation, planning practitioners have failed to fully realize the enabling power of physical space. Dominant models of disability, such as the medical abnormality and personal tragedy models are unjust and fail to address environmental inequity. The Independent Living Movement that began across several cities in the 1970s presented for the first time a socially and spatially just perspective of disability. This socio-spatial model was most clearly seen in the social and spatial justice campaigns of advocates living in Berkeley and featured in the Oscar-nominated feature documentary film Crip Camp. The way we imagine a social phenomenon or the models that we create to understand them have practical importance. The models or short-hand approaches we've built to understanding disability affect the way we build and construct the world around us. Thus, planning practitioners, researchers, and disability rights advocates will plan and create environments that can position access and equity at the center of a more developed relational and spatial model of justice.

Essentially, the way we relate to the physical environment is fundamentally constructed by the conceptions we have of "the other," who is operating or acting within and between specified geographies. Spatial justice not only can change the way we interact with our environment but more importantly how we relate to one another. How we situate bodily differences, functional impairments, age, gender, race, class, migration status, and sexual orientation, also impacts our physical, mental, and emotional health. This inherent insight that the social is spatial and the spatial is social is critical to understanding the too often silenced and overlooked experiences of individuals and communities that live on the margins. Our social contract to a great extent ignores a conceptualization of the injustice of space or the spatiality of injustice. A new social contract must center space so that we can reframe both the problems and the solutions to equity, access, and inclusion in human settlements.

But before reviewing how radical inclusion can shed light on how we can reimagine our conceptions of the other, let us review where these conceptions come from in the first place.

Implicit Bias

One side effect of socialization is that it tends to establish implicit biases. These reinforce stereotypes and influence our perceptions, judgments, decisions, and actions. Implicit bias is unconscious. It may even be different from your conscious belief system. Because our conscious brain cannot interpret all the information that we see, our initial instincts commonly are not based on fully processed interpretations, leading to a reliance on biases of some type. Over time, our personal experiences, memories, and the influence of socialization produce unconscious biases that at a basic level result in rapid categorization of others as either "like me" or "not like me." Implicit bias is therefore an automatic response in the brain in assigning a person to a group we have coded as "other." This leads to having reduced levels of interest and empathy for that person and forms the basis of prejudice and discrimination.

The literature suggests there are overlapping neural systems that link fear with certain groups who are coded as "other." At the neural level, the magnitude of implicit preferences for in-group and against out-group correlates with the activation of the amygdala.[10] The amygdala is a subcortical structure of the brain, part of the limbic system or the emotional brain, that has a major role in the "fight-flight response," and it becomes activated within a fraction of a second. The speed of this deeply embedded automatic response creates a response well before thoughts and actions based on the more reasoned part of the well-meaning person's brain.

Studies have demonstrated that our responses differ markedly between when we see or hear stimuli from people we consider in-group or out-group. Functional MRI (fMRI) results show that when individuals see facial images of people from a different ethnic background to their own, it often activates the amygdala more than seeing people of the same ethnicity. The way we respond to different accents can also be explained by amygdala response to in-group and out-group memberships. While hearing someone speaking with a similar accent elicits an enhanced neural response, repetition of another group's accent results in reduced neural responses.[11]

Implicit biases about persons with disabilities are pervasive and can lead to discrimination due to unfair or prejudicial treatment of people and groups. Implicit biases also tend to create spurious categorizations. For example, policymakers are prone to vulnerability bias and to consistently assume, based on their biases, that persons with disabilities can all be grouped together.[12] As a result, persons with disabilities tend to be overly represented by wheelchair users while underrepresented by persons with psychosocial disabilities, mental illness, chronic pain, immunocompromised individuals, or persons with learning, intellectual or invisible disabilities.

Implicit biases develop over the course of a lifetime, beginning at an early age. Empirical studies show a dominant preference or bias toward non-disabled bodies, often eliciting sympathy and pity toward persons with disabilities or making the false assumption that they are unhappy or

---

[10] https://nccc.georgetown.edu/bias/module-3/4.php

[11] https://blogs.scientificamerican.com/observations/what-neuroimaging-can-tell-us-about-our-unconscious-biases/

[12] Assumptions around vulnerability create the expectation that the vulnerability is inherent to the individual and not that the vulnerability is created through social structures and social conditioning. Too little attention is paid to the political, economic, and cultural positioning of vulnerability. The way this tends to manifest in reality is that people are *made* vulnerable by design. Vulnerability by design is therefore often unintentional but is still pervasive.

have a deep dissatisfaction with their life. To be sure, implicit biases cause us to see and judge people's traits as being more or less desirable or judge them as being more or less valuable to society. In this sense, changing our notion of what is justice becomes an inescapable starting point to challenge the pervasive power of implicit biases.

Justice as Fairness

We need to revisit the way we plan cities because it is becoming clear that adhering to best practices helps cities become more resilient places. More importantly, we must ensure inclusivity is at the heart of how we manage cities. We need to create a greater level of livability and embed inclusivity to ensure that everyone has equal access to housing and public spaces. We need to put people before profit. (Maimunah Mohd Sharif Under-Secretary-General and Executive Director of UN-Habitat)

Justice for people with disabilities is fundamentally a struggle for dignity, citizenship, and access. Under the dominant notions of justice, those who cannot produce value or who have impaired mental faculties are not understood to be full members of society. The capacity and capability of the so-called "weak" to exercise their rights, agency, and personhood still stands as a key litmus test in the definition of and struggle for justice.

Radical inclusion returns to the roots of justice, where scholars such as John Rawls in his *A Theory of Justice*[13] and *Justice as Fairness*[14] have put forward progressive ideas of justice centered around a fundamental belief that all people deserve to participate fully in every aspect of life. Rawls turned to the social contract tradition where justice is understood as the outcome of mutual advantage; i.e., that rules of justice are more beneficial for everyone than if each individual was to pursue their own advantage on their own. This presents several problematic areas for people living with disabilities. These areas fundamentally concentrate on the interaction between the individual and their environment.

One problem with contemporary theories of justice is that they are often based on "strong assumptions" that may introduce bias or exclude certain groups of people from the theory. For example, Martha Nussbaum

---

[13] Rawls, J. (1971). A Theory of Justice. *Cambridge: Belknap Press.*
[14] Rawls, J. (1958). Justice as Fairness. *The Philosophical Review,* 67(2), pp. 164–194.

and others argue that Rawls's theory is unable to account for our duties of justice toward the severely disabled (Sen 1980; Kittay 1999; Nussbaum 2006; Kittay and Carlson 2010). Indeed, Rawls's theory relies on a conception of justice that is based on the ability to participate in society, but this can exclude the severely disabled, who may not be able to participate in the same way as others, due to their cognitive or physical limitations. Consequently, people with disabilities may need additional resources and support to ensure their wellbeing and allow them to live with dignity. These critics challenge Rawls' purposeful exclusion of the severely disabled "non-normal" individuals from analysis. They further point out problems with the ability to constitute personhood and the inability to extend justice and rights to those that cannot care for themselves or whose cognitive capacities limit the capacity of making conscious decisions and being in active control of life.

In the social/human rights model, people are disabled by attitudes and environments that discriminate against them. They may have impairments of various kinds such as sensory, language, learning, or mobility impairments, but how disabled or enabled they are is a result of how environments are designed and how society responds. For example, a person may be strongly myopic (short-sighted), which is a relatively minor but still significant visual impairment. Are they disabled? No, society has made it easy for them to adjust as their glasses are affordable and readily available. Were this not so, driving, watching television, catching a bus, going to the cinema, or even identifying people in the street would be a challenge. They would, to a degree, be disabled. So do they "have a disability"? No. In this way, disability can be seen to be relational, not intrinsic. It depends on how society responds to the impairment. The socio-spatial model also necessitates the active participation of those who have been historically marginalized and excluded in shaping the requisite transformations.

I argue that a complete transformation of the structures that cause exclusion is fundamental to the field of urban planning, policy, and design. Too often justice has been relegated to philosophical experiments or narrow interpretations of laws. Radical inclusion expands this limited approach by offering a contextual understanding of human capabilities, which are routinely deprived by environmental design. These strategies, when applied in cities, reposition urban planning as an enabling force for expanding human agency, individual choice, freedom, and ultimately justice.

What Is Radical Inclusion?

Radical inclusion is about transformation from the inside out, not modification from the outside in. It involves creating an environment where accessibility and flexibility are so deeply embedded that special accommodations are rarely, if ever, needed, where the able-bodied person is no longer the normative standard, but one of a variety of types, and where the disabled person is no longer a problem in need of a solution, but a person whose lived experience and expertise open new ways of seeing and being for others. (Ele Chenier, Professor in the Department of History and Associate Professor in the Department of Gender, Sexuality, and Women's Studies, Simon Fraser University)

Simple inclusion leaves the structures responsible for the inequality and exclusion we see in the world today intact. Radical inclusion calls for a transformation of the structure itself. It is also useful to consider that the term radical comes from the Latin "radicalis," meaning "root." Therefore the term should not have connotations of extremes or simply the rejection of neoliberalism, but rather is focused on getting to the root of an issue or problem so that barriers are removed, people can express themselves fully, and their uniqueness be allowed to shine through. Radical inclusion means seeing everyone as equal, tackling the roots of inequality, and eliminating barriers to unlock human potential for all.

Radical inclusion is not about inserting persons with disabilities into existing structures, but about transforming systems to be inclusive of everyone. Inclusive communities put into place measures to support all people with disabilities or older persons at home, school, vocational centers, sports, cultural events, and in their communities. When barriers exist, inclusive communities transform the way they are organized to meet the needs of all people. Barriers create obstacles for individuals by denying or diminishing their choices. They may also deny or diminish fundamental human rights, such as political and public participation, employment, or education. Left unchecked, barriers perpetuate exclusion, isolation, disempowerment, poverty, and inequality.

The term "radical inclusion" has gained wider cultural awareness partially due to its inclusion as one of the Ten Principles of Burning Man. The principles were developed in 2004 by the festival co-founder Larry Harvey as a reflection of the community's ethos and culture as it had organically developed since the event's inception in the 1980s. Burning Man is a temporary city, constructed for one week each year (and subsequently deconstructed), located in the middle of the Black Rock Desert in Nevada with a population capped at 70,000 paying participants. It has forged a permanent community of people dedicated to celebrating creativity, self-expression, cultural differences, knowledge sharing, and releasing social stigma.[15] As it relates to Burning Man, radical inclusion states that anyone may be a part of the event and that no prerequisites exist for participation in the Burning Man community.

Radical inclusion is both a process and a goal to create the cities of tomorrow. When we consider how to achieve radical inclusion in our cities, if radical inclusion is the transformation of structures that caused exclusion, radically inclusive cities require a transformation of the systems in cities that promoted exclusion. For cities this means policies that encourage radical inclusion as well as targeted Universal Design that achieve it. There is a need for a new approach because of the context of the environments, trends, and issues that we as a global community are currently facing. This includes rapid urbanization and technological transformation of all parts of society, as well as the health, social, and economic upheaval caused by the COVID-19 pandemic. But how can disability justice theories and concepts of radical inclusion be advanced without a militant overthrow of the existing systems that are working? By building the world we want without destroying the one we already have.

DISABILITY JUSTICE AS A LENS FOR ADVANCING RADICAL INCLUSION

I have chosen to purposefully provide a broad notion of disability justice, one that is inclusive of a broader framework of disability rights, but at the same time expands it and makes it more relevant to our time. As a result, there could be other more narrow approaches, but here are five definitions that can help elucidate what disability justice is and how the term is applied in this book:

1. Disability justice is the recognition and promotion of the rights of people with disabilities to participate fully in society, and the dismantling of the barriers and discrimination that prevent them from doing so.

---

[15] https://www.higherlogic.com/blog/what-burning-mans-10-principles-can-teach-you-about-building-community/

2. Disability justice is a movement that seeks to create a world where people with disabilities are not only included, but also valued, respected, and celebrated for their unique perspectives and contributions.
3. Disability justice is an intersectional approach to addressing the complex interplay of ableism, racism, sexism, homophobia, and other forms of oppression experienced by people with disabilities, and working toward a more inclusive and equitable society.
4. Disability justice is the application of the principles of social justice to the rights and experiences of people with disabilities, with a focus on addressing the root causes of discrimination and inequality, and empowering individuals to live their lives to the fullest.
5. Disability justice is the recognition that disability is not a personal tragedy or individual deficit, but a natural part of the human experience that should be embraced and supported, rather than stigmatized and marginalized.

Each of the above definitions expands and builds on the evolving notion of disability as noted in the preamble of the UNCRPD. Disability justice thus has a relative salience that is contextualized within every city's particular norms, values,[16] and changing expectations. Further, the relative position of the notion should be explored in relation to the city's capability to respond to emerging issues and themes.

The disability justice movement builds upon the work of the disability rights movement, which has fought for decades to secure rights for disabled people and recognize their social position.[17] By taking a more context-specific approach, we can better understand how disabled people

[16] As opposed to a narrow, intersectional, and anti-capitalist approach to disability justice.

[17] For more clarification, I disagree with previous scholars that narrow the notion of disability justice. As I argue that disability justice is inseparable from the specific culture position of disability. As I have written before in my book, "Building the Inclusive City: Governance, Access and the Urban Transformation of Dubai" we should consider the salience or proclivity of various communities to adopt these rights. As such any contemporary urban approaches to disability justice should consider the position of each city's particular journey toward disability rights. Taking a more context-specific approach helps us understand the ways in which these communities and localities secured rights for disabled people, and others. Urban planners and future scholars should explore the specific ways by which they recognized the social position and the relative intersectionality of disabled people in their cities and the way varies intersectional identities may interact. The disability rights movement created the legal, political, and social preconditions for a disability justice movement to emerge.

in different cities and communities have secured their rights and how their experiences are shaped by other forms of marginalization. The disability rights movement has laid the groundwork for the emergence of a disability justice movement, a newer movement that centered the struggle of doubly marginalized by intersectional identities. Thus newer notions of disability justice are able to create the legal, political, cultural, and social preconditions for more culturally specific and holistic policy responses.

In order to go beyond the full participation of people with disabilities, that is to say their radical inclusion, it becomes indispensable to ensure that disability justice becomes part of institutional structures and is mature and ingrained in social norms. In turn, disability justice advocates for the removal of all forms of oppression thus revolving around all disabled people including "disabled people of color, immigrants with disabilities, queers with disabilities, trans and gender non-conforming people with disabilities, people with disabilities who are houseless, people with disabilities who are incarcerated, and people with disabilities who have had their ancestral lands stolen, amongst others."[18]

DEFINING RADICAL INCLUSION AS A FRAMEWORK FOR URBAN TRANSFORMATION

Radical inclusion is a framework that goes beyond simply promoting full participation and seeks to fundamentally transform systems in order to eliminate the agency deprivations that prevent individuals and communities from achieving their full potential. This approach recognizes that individuals and communities may be excluded or marginalized for a variety of reasons, including disability, race, gender, sexuality, and other forms of identity. Radical inclusion seeks to address these issues at their root, by creating inclusive systems that allow individuals and communities to exercise agency and make their own choices about how to live their lives. This approach recognizes that inclusive systems are essential for building more resilient and equitable societies and for unleashing the potential of all individuals and communities.

Disability justice implies the removal of all barriers as a concrete strategy to advancing radical inclusion. These can be in the form of physical, attitudinal, legal, regulatory, or policy barriers and can also simply be a

---

[18] Piepzna-Samarasinha, Leah Lakshmi (2018). *Care Work: Dreaming Disability Justice.* Vancouver, BC, Canada: Arsenal Pulp Press.

lack of information being available in accessible formats. No matter what form they take, these barriers prevent people from being able to fully and "radically" participate. Promoting equality of opportunities and access to services and information for persons with disabilities is also critical to strategies for reducing poverty and the effective realization of the Sustainable Development Goals (SDGs) and the shared objectives of the international community.

Disability justice is also one of the most powerful tools available in helping to advance spatial justice (Soja 1990; Harvey 2001). Because space is socially produced, it can therefore also be socially changed. The spatial shapes the social as much as the social shapes the spatial and spatial justice or injustice can be seen as both an outcome and a process.[19] There is no spatial justice without disability justice. Applying a disability lens to urban planning through historic eras creates an innovative multidisciplinary framework for understanding social and physical exclusion over time.

Distribution of space is an important aspect of realizing justice for disabled persons. It is only just if it is to the advantage of the least well-off stakeholder. Where environmental elements—and space itself—are conceived for the most part as fixed, immobile, and inflexible, planners may not see how their actions exercise a normalizing vision of physical ability that is socially constructed. Out of this notion a larger set of theories can be criticized and a new broader theory of justice can be formulated. If, however, disability is continuously held as a property of an individual independent of an environment, just theories of disability can never emerge.

The philosophies of the independent living movement and their political struggles have uncovered new truths about space and the inequity of its distribution but have not achieved the full potential possible with a spatial lens. Justice and democracy itself are at risk if spatial exclusion persists. Let the lessons learned and the struggles fought inform us and help us shape an open and more perfect union not just for people with disabilities but for everyone. My contribution is building on the literature by bringing into focus the enabling and disabling role of the environment and presenting disability justice as a tool to understand human agency more broadly, ultimately leading to the unlocking of capabilities through better design.

---

[19] https://www.jssj.org/wp-content/uploads/2012/12/JSSJ1-1en4.pdf

How Equity Relates to Justice

PolicyLink defines equity as "just and fair inclusion into a society in which all can participate, prosper, and reach their full potential. Unlocking the promise of the nation by unleashing the promise in us all."[20] Inclusiveness is a vital component of the digital transformation required to create more equitable and just cities. But equitable cities are about more than just providing access to new technologies, they extend right back to the basic planning and design decisions that occur throughout the development and expansion of cities.

Equity within cities forms part of the greater challenge to create social justice, by expanding opportunities for all persons, especially for persons with disabilities, older persons, or those who are adversely affected by policies that cause racial or economic exclusion. It is the responsibility of governments, institutions, decision makers, and city leaders to seek to reduce inequity by prioritizing the needs of those people in society who are routinely excluded from accessing urban environments or services within their cities.

Equity moves beyond notions of equality to incorporate policies that respond to difference. This has the effect of driving decision-making toward equitable policies that actively seek to reduce harm or exclusion of certain members of society. Equity is also intersectional in that there are a large number of overlaps between the pursuit of equitable cities and social justice and issues that affect community engagement and environmental issues.

Targeted Universalism as a Policy Tool for Radical Inclusion

Planning scholars and practitioners are powerful allies in promoting, protecting, and ensuring that persons with disabilities can exercise their rights and participate equally in city life. They play a key role in not only altering the built environment (i.e., removing unnecessary barriers) but also actively promoting the participation of persons with disabilities as a targeted underrepresented group.

Let us assume for simplicity that there are ten constraints reducing opportunities for group A, and two of those constraints are reducing opportunities for group B. If fifty percent of group A is constrained by 1

---

[20] American Planning Association https://www.planning.org/knowledgebase/equity/

and 2 and only ten percent of group B is constrained by 1 and 2, we might assume that since A is disproportionately constrained by 1 and 2, group A would disproportionately benefit from the removal of 1 and 2.

Suppose that the presence of any of the constraints is sufficient to deny opportunity. A universal policy that removed constraints 1 and 2 would vastly increase the opportunity movement of group B. It would not, however, change the conditions of group A because there are still eight remaining constraints reducing opportunity for that group. Yet the failure of group A to translate the policy into opportunity might be seen as a failure on the part of group A, and not a failure of policy.

What this false universalism fails to address is that groups of people are differently situated in relation to institutional and policy dynamics. If one only looks at one or two constraints, one is likely to inaccurately assume that groups who are in very different circumstances are in fact similar. The flaw in this false universalism is not overcome by anti-discrimination policies. One could argue that the disfavored group is not being discriminated against in a traditional sense. Instead, their situatedness is causing the disadvantage. It is important and appropriate to remove the institutional and situational constraints of group A. This is the universal part of the effort. But it is equally important to remove the additional constraints that are experienced by group B. This is the targeted part of the effort. Failure to do so in issues related to race will not only reproduce racialized disparities, it will also continue to support divisive racialized meaning and discourse.

THE NEW REALITY

The future is accessible and radically diverse. This future is within reach. We are imagineers for the future we want to build, and there are new ideas and technologies emerging that are producing solutions that result in faster, better, and cheaper outcomes. The way we perceive the problem—*is the problem.* A problem is an invitation to reimagine, innovate, and lead the way to radical inclusion. Together we are catalysts to a more accessible and inclusive future.

Cities define urban life as the collection of places where social groups interact with or ignore one another; where order and resistance meet. Urban planning must be repositioned as an enabling force for expanding human agency, individual choice, and freedom. New models can be created and lives changed by lowering barriers to participation, redressing social exclusion, and empowering individuals to be active in civic life.

These models and changes are not uniform, there will be variations from city to city, state to state, and country to country.

Every human life has value, but during that life most people will also encounter many obstacles. At the same time, every human life has limitless potential. Every place or every person is endowed with possibilities and particularities that make that place or person unique. The challenge is to understand the real barriers and remove them at their root so that physical and human potential can be unlocked. The future is urban, with cities that are accessible and radically diverse. The future is within reach.

Emerging Approaches to Radical Inclusion in Practice

What is the extent to which radical inclusion is an inescapable imperative for cities? How do we better understand and evaluate governance within cities? In previous sections we explored how radical inclusion can advance governance and how crucial it is to transforming our current institutions. The following sections help us create performance criteria for advancing resilient and responsive systems of the future. The creation of radically inclusive practices offers functional and emotional benefits to city and team leaders, policymakers, and other urban stakeholders looking to implement measures to improve the accessibility and resilience of their cities.

When implemented correctly radical inclusion can:

1. **Eliminate individual and group agency deprivations**
    (a) Unlock human potential and enhance individual agency through more holistic policies and broad based governance
    (b) Collectively empower marginalized groups, to foster more socially resilient and cohesive societies
    (c) Create accountability mechanisms to lower discrimination and social friction through an integrated, evidence based, capability enhancing approach to urban policy
2. **Inspire individuals and organizations to achieve new goals**
    (a) Help foster growth in under-appreciated resources such as human capital, social capital, knowledge capital, and a new unaccounted resource—inspirational capital

(b) New forms of capital accumulation can generate greater wealth and social wellbeing
(c) Explicit and continuous learning, capacity building, and empowerment
(d) Measure productivity and creativity in the workplace and community at large
(e) Belief and pride that cities can work better for everyone
(f) Demonstrate through effective benchmarking that diversity, equity, access, and inclusion are demonstrably creating a world that's better for all of us
(g) Help create tangible, validated, and proven tools to unlock underutilized resources and drive investments for an inclusive transformation agenda

3. **Data, monitoring, and evaluation criteria drive impact**

    (a) Integrated measures drive progress on ESG and capital accounting
    (b) Increase confidence from the fact that these goals are measurable, stakeholders are accountable to paving the way toward common goals, and are committed to building a radically inclusive future
    (c) New data, monitoring and evaluation criteria can create a roadmap toward an inclusive future

In conclusion, the adoption of emerging approaches to radical inclusion in urban planning can have a transformative impact on marginalized communities. By eliminating agency deprivations and promoting social cohesion, cities can empower these groups and unlock their potential, leading to increased productivity and creativity in the workplace, as well as lower discrimination and social friction. By demonstrating the tangible benefits of diversity, equity, access, and inclusion, cities can also inspire individuals and organizations to achieve new goals and create more inclusive and resilient societies. The next chapters will offer more insights into how these approaches are applied and elaborate on implications for their greater adoption.

CALLOUT BOX—NEWS ARTICLE

The importance of ensuring inclusive and accessible public spaces
Source: Open Access Government

Consider This What some social commentators call "social cleansing still does go on," acknowledged a local government planner. Neighbors describe the eviction of a homeless person from public spaces in his London borough as heartless. While accessible public spaces have always been limited by rules, the regulations that set out who can enter and what is permitted within are frequently challenged. As public spaces are used in a variety of ways, governments and organizations responsible for managing them respond by rewriting the terms of access to those spaces through new laws and regulations. In this way, the rules of access to public space are essentially mediated by organizations with more power and then tested, questioned, or contested by those with less.

These types of issues are important because the accessibility and inclusivity of public spaces is an important aspect of a city's culture and democracy. Public spaces play a crucial role in fostering a sense of community and enabling people to participate in the social and political life of the city. It is therefore important to ensure that public spaces are designed, managed, and regulated in a way that promotes accessibility and inclusivity for all members of the community.

There are also implications related to the privatization of public spaces, where accessibility issues arise if private entities are responsible for managing and maintaining the space. In these cases, there is a heightened risk that the private owners or land managers may prioritize their own interests and agendas over the needs of the broader public. This can result in exclusionary practices, such as the eviction of homeless people or the displacement of persons with disabilities, for example by making it harder for people with mobility limitations to access certain areas.

References

Agarwal, P. (2020, April 12). What neuroimaging can tell us about our unconscious biases. *Scientific American*. https://blogs.scientificamerican.com/observations/what-neuroimaging-can-tell-us-about-our-unconscious-biases/

American Planning Association. (n.d.). *Social Equity*. Knowledgebase Collection. https://www.planning.org/knowledgebase/equity/

Burning Man Project. (n.d.). *The 10 Principles of Burning Man*. https://burningman.org/culture/philosophical-center/

Chenier, E. (2020). *Radical Inclusion: Equity and Diversity Among Female Faculty at Simon Fraser University*. Academic Women of SFU. https://www2.unbc.

ca/sites/default/files/sections/equity-diversity-inclusion/radicalinclusion-aug312020.pdf

Cities for All Training Program. (2020, November 27). *Module Two: Non-Discrimination*. https://cities4all.org/wp-content/uploads/2020/12/C4A-Training-Program-Modules-2-Final.pdf

Georgetown University National Center for Cultural Competence. (n.d.). *Conscious & Unconscious Biases in Health Care*. https://nccc.georgetown.edu/bias/module-3/4.php

Golby, A. J., Gabrieli, J. D. E., Chiao, J. Y., & Eberhardt, J. L. (2001). Differential responses in the fusiform region to same-race and other-race faces. *Nature Publishing Group*. https://web.stanford.edu/~eberhard/downloads/200108-DifferentialResponses.pdf

Graham, G., Ostrowski, M., & Sabina, A. (2015, August 6). Defeating the ZIP code health paradigm: Data, technology, and collaboration are key. *Health Affairs*. https://www.healthaffairs.org/do/10.1377/forefront.20150806.049730

Harvey, D. (1973). *Social Justice and the City*. University of Georgia Press.

Kristof, N. (2015, May 7). Our Biased Brains. *New York Times*. https://www.nytimes.com/2015/05/07/opinion/nicholas-kristof-our-biased-brains.html

Lefebvre, H. (1998). *The Right to the City*.

Phelps, E. A., O'Connor, K. J., Cunningham, W. A., Funayama, E. S., Gatenby, J. C., Gore, J. C., & Banaji, M. R. (2000). Performance on Indirect Measures of Race Evaluation Predicts Amygdala Activation. *Journal of Cognitive Neuroscience*, *12*(5), 729–738. https://doi.org/10.1162/089892900562552

Piepzna-Samarasinha, L. L. (2018). *Care work: Dreaming disability justice*. Arsenal Pulp Press.

Pineda, V. (2016, August 22). Building a City of Radical Inclusion. *Hostfully*. https://travel.hostfully.com/building-a-city-of-radical-inclusion-d14ba7e1aa0f

Soja, E. W. (2009). The City and Spatial Justice. *Spatial Justice*. https://www.jssj.org/wp-content/uploads/2012/12/JSSJ1-1en4.pdf

Pineda, V. (2008). Enabling Justice: Spatializing Disability in the Built Environment. *Critical Planning Journal*, *15*(Summer), 111–123. https://scholar.google.com/citations?view_op=view_citation&hl=en&user=nZ16Ss8AAAAJ&citation_for_view=nZ16Ss8AAAAJ:u5HHmVD_uO8C

Rawls, J. (1971). *A Theory of Justice*. Belknap Press.

Rawls, J. (1958). Justice as Fairness. *The Philosophical Review*, *67*(2), 164–194.

Open Access This chapter is licensed under the terms of the Creative Commons Attribution 4.0 International License (http://creativecommons.org/licenses/by/4.0/), which permits use, sharing, adaptation, distribution and reproduction in any medium or format, as long as you give appropriate credit to the original author(s) and the source, provide a link to the Creative Commons licence and indicate if changes were made.

The images or other third party material in this chapter are included in the chapter's Creative Commons licence, unless indicated otherwise in a credit line to the material. If material is not included in the chapter's Creative Commons licence and your intended use is not permitted by statutory regulation or exceeds the permitted use, you will need to obtain permission directly from the copyright holder.

CHAPTER 4

How Cities Shape Our Experience

Abstract Cities need to be places of inclusion, belonging, and access. Failing to do so leads to social and economic costs for citizens, such as the marginalization and exclusion of persons with disabilities and older persons from participating in important services and activities. The construction industry shapes our built environment and has a significant role to play in ensuring cities are places of inclusion and access to create a more equitable future for us all. However, current practices within the construction industry are failing to accommodate persons with disabilities and older persons. Inclusive practices in construction management require technical approaches that support project delivery. The construction industry can inform and support policy objectives, but it is lacking in its management approach to ensure accessibility for all. There is a need for integrated approaches that are embedded in the standard operating procedures of cities, companies, and the wider construction industry to absorb the costs of accessibility over the life cycle of building or infrastructure developments. City leaders and construction companies must engage local communities in participatory planning and share effective processes and best practices for incorporating accessibility principles into their projects.

Keywords Construction industry • Urban future • Radical inclusion • Social and economic cost • Inclusive practices • Construction management • Best practices • Participatory planning

The challenges of the new society are the challenges of the city. The majority of the world's population already lives in cities and this proportion only continues to rise. Therefore, cities are places where all the challenges and contradictions of the social human system emerge. Cities are where we witness everything in its most exaggerated manner—all the different conflicts of society. Whether we are talking about the future of work or the future of the social contract, all of the big issues are perfectly represented in the new urban reality. (Joan Clos, Former Executive Director of UN Habitat, Former Mayor of Barcelona)

At the age of ten, three years after moving to the United States and my parents' divorce, I was preparing to meet up with my father. I clearly remember my mother choosing New York City as the backdrop to this encounter. The physical and spatial embodiment of liberty, opportunity, and prosperity were values that my mother sought to highlight as she convinced my father that it was necessary to my development for our family to permanently move and set roots in Newport Beach, at the time one of the most accessible and affluent cities in California.

Through my mother's insistence and geographical intention, I came to understand that cities are the embodiment of our values, a representation of a community's collective imagination. Cities agglomerate people's wants, needs, priorities, failures, and successes. By the time I reconnected with my father in New York that hot summer, I had already lived in or visited family in many diverse urban centers. Caracas, Geneva, Newport Beach, and Belgrade each held a piece of my home, each had roots, and each had meaning. Each hometown was so different. Each carried a legacy of what the community valued. Each was built, inhabited, used, and maintained in wildly different ways.

Most historians and social scientists treat cities as mere settings. In fact, urban places play a far greater role and are pivotal in shaping our experiences.[1] Each of the above cities shaped my own experience, my understanding of the world around me, and ultimately my understanding of myself. Each city (and its citizens) held different assumptions of who the city was built for and how I could function. In bigger cities daily life has a faster, artificial rhythm and, for good and ill, people and agencies affect each other through externalities (uncompensated effects) whose impact is inherently geographical.

---

[1] Harris, R. (2021) How Cities Matter. Cambridge: *Cambridge University Press (Elements in Global Urban History). doi: 10.1017/9781108782432.*

Richard Harris (2021) addresses this by saying, "In economic terms, urban concentration enables efficiency and promotes innovation while raising the costs of land, housing, and labor. Socially, it can alienate or provide anonymity, while fostering new forms of community. It creates congestion and pollution, posing challenges for governance. Some effects extend beyond urban borders, creating cultural change." The character of cities varies by country and world region, but it has generic qualities, a claim best tested by comparing places that are most different. These qualities intertwine, creating built environments that endure. To fully comprehend such path dependency, we need to develop a synthetic vision that is historically and geographically informed.

This is the urban century. Half of humanity already lives in towns and cities and it is projected that within the next 50 years, more than two-thirds of the planet's population will be urbanized. Forecasts show the overall growth of the world's population and the ongoing shift of people moving from rural to urban areas will add another 2.5 billion people to cities by 2050.[2] This rate of urbanization translates to more than 87 million people moving into cities each year. But of the 4 billion people globally living in cities, one third of them live in slums. The rapid pace in which people are moving into cities will force everyone from city leaders and urban planners to those of us who simply call cities home to consider the consequences of failing to provide healthy, safe, and accessible environments to all the current and future inhabitants of the world's cities. Our understanding of the core values of cities and evolving priorities of average citizens are shaping the broader and farther-reaching array of choices we make about the cities we inhabit. These choices are more consequential now than at any time in history.

THE COST OF EXCLUSION AND THE POWER OF IMAGINARY CITIES

Cities have the potential to accelerate the main premise of this book, radical inclusion, and do so by unlocking human agency and shaping human flourishing.[3] The ideas around human development, human agency, and

---

[2] United Nations, Department of Economic and Social Affairs, Population Division, (2018). *2018 Revision of the World Urbanization Prospects.* https://esa.un.org/unpd/wup/

[3] The idea of flourishing has a long history, coming from Aristotle (where it is called eudaimonia). A life of eudaimonia is **a life in which one fulfills one's potential as a human being.**

human flourishing are vital to the way we imagine cities and construct civic life. Cities, towns, and human settlements shape our interactions and these interactions shape the way one fulfills one's potential as a human being.

This is, first and foremost, a matter of justice. And the capabilities approach, developed under Amartya Sen and Martha Nussbaum, provides a mechanism for measuring justice in terms of a place's "ability to secure to citizens a list of central capabilities"[4] (Nussbaum 2007, p. 281). Thinking in terms of capabilities allows for the assessment of whether a society is truly just and equal.

The ramifications of poor urban planning are severe. Poor urban planning exacerbates inequality through capability deprivations. Poor urban planning increases inequality by preventing some citizens from being able to fully participate in public life, while affording others with relative privileges by design. That people with disabilities, for example, are *allowed* to work in any given country means little if the streets prevent wheelchair users from accessing them, if buses are unable to accommodate them, if workplaces fail to provide appropriate sick leave, and so on. The same is true when considering all nature of rights and opportunities: the right to education, to marry, to have children, etc. Especially in very large cities located in developing countries, informal developments can increase the marginalization of resident populations by crowding people together, restricting mobility, and consequently depriving persons with disabilities their wellbeing, dignity, and the benefits of social and economic development on an equal basis with others. So far, poorly planned cities create a range of physical and digital barriers, limiting access to information and mobility options. They deprive human capabilities, increase vulnerability to environmental hazards, and exclude people from accessing services.

Human agency is one of the main reasons cities thrive but with the wrong approaches human agency (free laissez faire market approaches) can also accelerate and obstruct radical inclusion. Cities can set the rules and adopt standards that enhance human capabilities. Over the past few years (think of remote work) we have seen an immediate economic impact on the lives of their inhabitants (especially persons with significant disabilities who are returning to work in greater numbers). Urban policies and municipal services play a crucial role in unlocking human agency and in

---

[4] Nussbaum, Martha C. (2007). Frontiers of Justice: Disability, Nationality, Species Membership. In *Frontiers of Justice*. Harvard University Press. https://doi.org/10.4159/9780674041578.

turn shaping human flourishing. Cities thus become testaments to their times and carry legacies as the physical manifestation of the social values of the period. For all their inhabitants, cities serve as centers of life, economic activity, and community. In fulfilling this role, cities become *places of belonging* and the inability to access your city indicates first and foremost that city leaders don't believe you belong.[5]

How we think about cities and the people that inhabit them shape the way they are built and how they are used.[6] What we choose to fund, build, demolish, and redesign indicates what we value and, if not properly done, can be detrimental to city dwellers' life and human agency. Failing to retrofit old and inaccessible public transportation, for example, indicates that city leaders don't believe that the mobility of the elderly and the disabled is a worthy priority.

Urban settlements on aggregate are better than rural settlements in affording diverse individual choices, and the capacity to act and interact with others (much different than themselves). Human flourishing goes beyond simply exercising choices with the aim of influencing the individual's life conditions and chances. Human flourishing can be understood as an effort to find fulfillment and realize one's individual potential in the context of a larger society, each with the right to do the same.[7] While urbanization offers to unlock human potential as it brings forward economic and social benefits, it also brings significant demographic, political, and equity challenges. The development of new and expanded urban environments results in infrastructure, programs, and services with the capability to either enable or impede the participation of some members of society. These challenges must be overcome by ensuring that belonging is designed into cities as they evolve into the smart cities of tomorrow. There is a need for city leaders and planners to put in place policies and planning

---

[5] Schweik, S (2010). The Ugly Laws: Disability in Public. *NYU Press.*

[6] For further reading on explicit exclusion of certain groups of people from urban life, see literature on segregation, apartheid, and for references on the experiences of persons with disabilities, see literature and writing by Susan Schweik on "ugly laws."

[7] The idea of vulnerability is born out of the insight that human beings are soft and capable of being wounded. Human flourishing embraces our shared humanity and serves everyone's interest. Humans are both fragile and resilient. Human flourishing is both the optimal continuing development of human beings' potentials and living well as a human being, which means being engaged in relationships and activities that are meaningful, that is aligned with both their own values and humanistic values, in a way that is satisfying to them. Rooted in Aristotelian ethics, it values health intrinsically and applies universally to all human lives.

principles that ensure the most vulnerable people in society aren't left behind.

Making Imaginary Cities Real

Well planned urban settlements afford their citizens access to economic opportunities, cultural experiences, and community, in large part due to the talents, resources, desires, and interests of individuals working together. What happens then, when the only way to access a city's services is by owning and operating a car, or when getting fresh vegetables from a neighborhood market necessitates navigating around missing or broken sidewalks, or through unsafe roads or dangerous intersections? What does it mean when a city's services, resources, or even technological advances leave behind those who could most benefit from them? Or perhaps, more importantly, how can we strengthen the capacities of cities to leave no one behind, to lock no one out of progress and success?

To answer these questions and realize the radical inclusion in cities of tomorrow, city officials, developers, planners, and regular citizens should consider the factors shaping cities now, from climate change, to urbanization, to the rise of global pandemics. In order to imagine what a safe, resilient, smart, and radically inclusive city could look like we have to understand why our concept of the city matters now more than any time in history.

In this chapter, I contend that cities matter because the future of humanity will be won or lost in cities, and specifically in the manner in which radical inclusion will shape the legacy of this urban century. This chapter will first explore why this is delving into what it means for a city to be a place of inclusion, belonging, and access, but more importantly we will explore the social and economic costs of cities that fail to work for their citizens by exploring how the ubiquity of urban barriers deprive persons with disabilities[8] and older persons of their fundamental rights, and further marginalize or exclude large segments of the population from participating equally in health services, employment, education, or social protective services. This chapter concludes with a few key points on how and why to apply radically inclusive strategies in the urban century. It will also explore how major crises, such as a global health pandemic, can impact the

---

[8] Pineda, V (2008). Enabling Justice: Spatializing Disability in the Built Environment. *Critical Planning Journal 15 (2008): 111–23.*

functioning of cities and the services they provide for the world's billions of urban residents.

The Influence and Shortcomings of the Construction Industry

The construction industry plays an important role in helping to shape a more equitable urban future. In fact, construction was one of the first businesses that humans developed. We are largely reliant on it for our accommodation, places of work, transportation, and recreation. The built environment is constructed in a great part by the practices, values, norms, and operating guidelines of the construction industry. But the current set of standardized processes within the construction industry is failing persons with disabilities and older persons. The impact of this failure continues to carry significant costs to all stakeholders interested in building a more inclusive and sustainable urban future.

Construction management is a discipline of practices and processes that enable the delivery of projects, programs, and entire elements (like neighborhoods, economic zones, and infrastructure) of the built environment. Construction management can be regarded as the practical application and convergence of policy intentions (economic, social, and political) and delivers elements of such policies in the built environment. For older persons and persons with disabilities, inclusive practices in construction management require technical approaches that support overall project delivery. It is an essential professional service that has extensive connections to other subject fields such as planning, design, and operation within the built environment sector.

The construction industry can inform and support policy objectives and design specifications (such as Universal Design) by engaging fully in the planning, design, and pre-construction process with all stakeholders. The construction industry can share field and project management experience in the design, constructability, and usability of important accessibility features and design standards in construction, design, and delivery of vital public infrastructure.

Construction management is the important process that considers both the macro and micro sphere of the entire lifecycle of the built environment. The macro sphere of construction management covers issues at the national or international level such as industry statistics, analysis, and projections on codes and standards, building information management, procurement and contracts, supply networks, workforce productivity, and workplace health and safety. The micro sphere of construction management considers specific issues related to the delivery of projects such as feasibility studies, cost plans, design justification, process schedules, risk assessments, quality and traceability assurance, productivity analysis, service level agreements, and post occupancy evaluation.[9]

But one area where construction management is severely lacking at both the macro and micro sphere level is a management approach that is inclusive of all people—no matter their age or functional limitations—and of the legal mandates to ensure that spaces are accessible and useful to the public. There is no explicit mention of "managing" accessibility in the construction management process. For major infrastructure developments, the operation and maintenance costs (commonly referred to as O&M) over the lifetime of an asset is in the range of 40–80 percent of the initial construction costs to build the asset. While the O&M costs accrue over many years or decades after completion of the initial build, these O&M cost components are largely determined early on, during the design and engineering phase.

Nevertheless, no one is taking ownership of accessibility in this space and as a consequence many costly and mission critical mistakes are occurring. While designing in accessibility costs around 2 percent of total design and construction cost, a retrofit can increase construction costs from 10–200 percent of original costs. There is a criminal lack of management experience and oversight. If we don't intentionally manage inclusion in construction management, we accidentally reproduce exclusion, we reproduce barriers, we reproduce gaps and costly mistakes.

Asset Management and Participatory Planning

Asset managers are assigned to manage the costs of maintenance for each city asset, so in the case of a new public precinct development this might include park benches, lampposts, cross walks, curb cuts, public buildings, and all other assets within these public buildings. Asset managers also develop or oversee the development of recommendations on prioritized strategic maintenance and capital project programs for city infrastructure

---

[9] Chen, Z. (2019). Grand challenges in construction management. *Frontiers in Built Environment*, 5(31). Available from: https://doi.org/10.3389/fbuil.2019.00031.

using historical, current use, condition, replacement cost, maintenance costs, and other data consistent with asset management principles and best practices. They also ensure the safety of these assets and the work carried out, yet do not monitor the accessibility of these assets.

Asset management refers to a planned approach for managing and investing in a municipality's infrastructure. But in the status quo, this doesn't extend to incorporating accessibility. As anticipated above, incorporating accessibility from the outset and addressing all phases of the project life cycle should be viewed as a vital risk mitigation and cost saving measure for cities committed to accessibility and inclusion. By including accessibility in the initial design considerations rather than adding them as an afterthought, this ensures an integrated approach to the final usability and long-term impact of the project that benefits people through the human life cycle of all ages and abilities.

So the term, "build it in, don't bolt it on," has real significance to efficient infrastructure design and construction. This point took center stage at a recent discussion with the head of asset management in the Department of Municipalities and Transport of Abu Dhabi, where we realized that this was a big opportunity; a way to understand assets in an entirely new way. A way to also assess the costs of exclusion and the cost savings of accessible products and accessible assets.

In every construction project there are trade-offs. Neither physical infrastructure nor the construction industry exist in the theoretical space of policy, but in the nuts and bolts, where the rubber meets the road. There will always be difficult decisions to make in terms of design specifications, budgets, operations, supply chains, access reviews, project timelines, staffing, and usability testing. However, an integrated approach that is embedded in the standard operating procedures of the city, company, or industry allows costs such as those associated with designing in accessibility to be absorbed and amortized over the life cycle of a project.

City planners, leaders, and the companies that construct our urban infrastructure and environments must engage local communities via participatory planning to ensure ongoing community involvement initiatives during the planning and design stage of urban developments. Major companies working in the construction industry need to cooperate with one another to share effective processes and best practices that lead to efficient and effective incorporation of accessibility principles. A good example of this is the Considerate Constructors Scheme, which is a nonprofit, independent organization founded by the United Kingdom's construction industry to share stakeholder engagement, accessibility, and sustainability best practices.

There is a clear opportunity here, as the construction industry is notoriously slow to adopt many of the latest technological and social innovations that have been far more rapidly integrated into other industries. So as the construction industry is still evolving to take onboard the opportunities presented by digital transformation and new technologies such as 3D printing, there is also scope for the industry to embed accessibility processes in the same manner that safety considerations have been integrated into the construction management process in the past. Each of these trends could have a massive impact on increasing participation and inclusion of persons with disabilities and older persons into daily life. There is still much progression and maturity yet to occur in the industry, so our time is now. Those leaders and early adopters that successfully operationalize accessibility and inclusion will have the opportunity to shape industry wide standards that everyone else will follow.

How the Pandemic Highlighted the Need for Integrated Approaches

The pandemic has highlighted gaps of legislation, public policies, and effective measures. It has highlighted lack of accessibility to hospitals, health care, and information. During quarantine there was lack of access to food and essential services and difficulties in the exercise of human rights such as education and work. The solution to these problems is universal accessibility. (Maria Soledad Cisternas Special Envoy of the UN Secretary-General on Disability and Accessibility)

Much has been written about the pandemic's impact on urban planning. The pandemic accelerated existing trends such as increasing rates of urbanization, digital transformation, climate change, and the inadequacy of our global health systems.[10] As my friend Emilia Saiz, Secretary General of United Cities and Local Governments, likes to remind me, "Cities are on the front lines of global development, this is more evident each day, we cannot solve global challenges without more integrated local approaches. The ways in which we develop solutions matter now more than ever. The

---

[10] Anderson, J., Rainie, L. and Vogels, E.A., (2021). Experts say the "new normal" in 2025 will be far more tech-driven, presenting more big challenges. *Pew Research Center, 18.*

COVID-19 pandemic, including the responses to it, demonstrated a serious threat to global health, the provision of city services, and the livelihood and wellbeing of billions." Findings from the Equity and Access Learning Series, co-organized by UCLG, GIZ, and World Enabled found that containment measures themselves actually threatened the lives of some of the nearly 550 million persons with disabilities and older persons that live in urban areas when for instance many people became cut off from access to vital home or specialist health services. The imposed limitations on mobility, participation, expression, and social interactions had unprecedented political, economic, and social implications.

The COVID-19 outbreak was a universal global phenomenon, yet saw a wide range of responses. All countries were forced to prepare, respond, and recover, but each did so in a different way. However, for cities and towns in low- and middle-income countries, the pandemic presented a greater challenge due to weaker health care systems and lack of social safety nets. These challenges were amplified again for cities that host large populations of refugees and displaced people, either living in camps or squatting in slums and low-income settlements in urban areas. The large metro regions in the United States faced similar challenges, such as in New York City, Chicago, and Los Angeles where the hardest hit neighborhoods consisted predominantly of low-income Black and Latino residents.

The forces that control the ability for people to participate in their cities and people's wellbeing in general have also been exacerbated by the COVID-19 pandemic.[11] It has exposed areas of weakness within institutions and services that become absolute priorities for people facing immediate concerns. The pandemic presented us with a range of responses in different cities around the world, some that proved far more successful than others. It also presented us with the opportunity to decide what our new normal is—do we simply want to go back to how things were before?

Many of the impacts of the pandemic caused distortions to background urbanization trends by altering the population growth rates or the areas

---

[11] Impacts were not evenly distributed across neighborhoods and populations. Those living in poor conditions were at higher risk of serious complications, they were also disproportionately affected. People who were above 60 years of age and also living with disabilities experienced higher risk due to existing health conditions. This can be exacerbated by having limited or restricted mobility, limited access to health centers, limited access to social services and poor spatial planning. Having limited access to resources and communications is also highly problematic as many at-risk people cannot access mainstream media and communications channels. Many also have limited social networks to provide physical and social support.

where people wanted to reside. In the United States, there was a marked decrease in urban growth, evident by 39 out of 48 core counties in major US metropolitan areas showing lower population growth in 2019–20 than in 2018–19.[12,13] This population slowdown in major metropolitan areas was partially due to deaths, lower birth rates, decreased immigration from abroad, and out-migration of existing residents. More wealthy people chose to leave the cities for the suburbs, especially as remote working possibilities were broadened. At the same time, a high proportion of immigrants were entering cities. Remote working opportunities throughout the pandemic have worsened the gap between wealthy and low-income workers, contributing to higher rates of COVID-19 infections in low-income communities. The Economic Policy Institute found that 61 percent of workers in the highest income quartile had access to remote work opportunities, compared to just 9 percent of workers in the lowest income quartile.[14]

In addition to remote working, some of the most important trends that have emerged during the pandemic and in response to the crisis include an increased strain on digital infrastructure and reduced data privacy for citizens. It has also seen greater growth of local decentralized systems and networks, support for open innovation, and a shift to participatory, virtual cultural experiences. By recognizing the emergence of these trends and taking measures to understand their likely impacts, it is possible to integrate the positives that they may provide in the post-COVID world. Accelerated digital transformations as a consequence of meeting the demands of the pandemic can be used as a tool for creating more inclusive cities.

The large element of the unknown and need for rapid response created situations in cities around the world where various trial and error type approaches were taken and encouraged greater innovation in response

---

[12] Pineda, V.S. and Corburn, J., (2020). Disability, urban health equity, and the coronavirus pandemic: promoting cities for all. *Journal of Urban Health, 97(3), pp. 336–341.*

[13] William H. Frey, (2021). Pandemic Population Change across Metro America: Accelerated Migration, Less Immigration, Fewer Births and More Deaths. May 20, 2021. https://www.brookings.edu/research/pandemic-population-change-across-metro-america-accelerated-migration-less-immigration-fewer-births-and-more-deaths/

[14] Gould, E and Shierholtz, H. (2023). Not Everybody Can Work from Home: Black and Hispanic Workers Are Much Less Likely to Be Able to Telework. *Economic Policy Institute (blog)*, accessed May 16, 2023, https://www.epi.org/blog/black-and-hispanic-workers-are-much-less-likely-to-be-able-to-work-from-home/

protocols. We know that this won't be the last pandemic nor the last crisis that cities around the world will face. Therefore there is a strong need for the future-proofing of our cities against these types of major disruptions. But by measuring the impacts of various strategies and protocols, retaining what works and discarding what doesn't, it allows cities and individuals to maintain a spirit of continuous and permanent innovation that can help us rebuild our cities and societies to be more resilient and more inclusive in the future.

CHALLENGES AND OPPORTUNITIES IN BUILDING BELONGING BY DESIGN

It is time to stop allowing ourselves to be characterized as vulnerable. As liabilities in emergencies and disasters. Vulnerability is due to failures in providing accessibility in the built environment, failures in providing effective communications access, and failures in emergency and disaster programs. (Marcie Roth, CEO of World Institute on Disability, Former Director for Disability, Federal Emergency Management Administration (FEMA))

The pandemic was an unprecedented collective moment. Many city leaders that I spoke to understood the importance of the immediacy of collective decision-making. To support them, the organization I run, World Enabled, created an unprecedented pandemic response program that linked city leaders via WhatsApp groups. Over 25,000 resources were shared over 24 months. A network of over 2000 advocates and civic leaders were able to share what was working in real time. They were collectively learning how to construct the new normal. They were rapidly prototyping inclusive pandemic responses, and in the process—shaping the future.

The stigma against persons with disabilities that characterizes us as vulnerable was one of the most dangerous elements of the pandemic. Throughout the pandemic, the fact that health officials made decisions regarding the rationing of medical and other supplies based on who was deemed most valuable was highly problematic. According to an article entitled, "Disability Discrimination, Medical Rationing and COVID-19" the reported rise in the number of "do not resuscitate" orders being imposed on people with disabilities has "caused particular concerns from a human rights perspective."[15] in New York and Kansas, for example, medical providers received guidelines indicating that ventilators should be removed "from people using them for a chronic condition who are judged lower priority, in order to give them to other individuals."[16] These types of decisions disregard the safety and autonomy of disabled people who rely on ventilators for chronic health conditions and demonstrate how the lives of non-disabled people are prioritized over those with disabilities. Similarly, a National Public Radio investigation found that throughout the pandemic, disabled and elderly people in Oregon were repeatedly denied ventilators and pressured to sign Do Not Resuscitate orders.[17] Decisions like this, which are made on the assumption that persons with disabilities and older people are inherently vulnerable and necessarily have lower quality of life, are both extraordinarily common and extremely dangerous.

The intersection of poverty and inequality is most evident and visible in cities. Therefore targeted policies and actions are needed to respond to such impacts. Especially for the most vulnerable. These policies need to be data-driven, including disaggregated data on persons with disabilities so that responses can be developed that have fully considered data on barriers and improving accessibility. The current trend in the world of statistics is to rely on technology to administer survey questions, rather than using humans in the field. We know that people with disabilities and the elderly are far less likely to be able to access the technology that would enable them to respond to online surveys or telephone surveys. This means that even disaggregated data on persons with disabilities may fail to include the experiences of many disabled people. Groups involved in these processes are urged to work closely with disabled persons' and older persons' organizations so that researchers may understand more effective ways to collect data on these groups. This further ensures their perspectives are taken into account when determining which responses need to be prioritized.

When persons with disabilities have full access and are included at the table before, during, and after disasters, they can be contributors and true

---

[15] Chen, B and McNamara, D, M. (2020). Disability Discrimination, Medical Rationing and COVID-19. *Asian Bioethics Review 12, no. 4 (2020): 511–18,* https://www.ncbi.nlm.nih.gov/pmc/articles/PMC7471485/

[16] *ibid.*

[17] Shapiro, J. (2020). As Hospital Fear Being Overwhelmed by COVID-19, Do the Disabled Get the Same Access?" *National Public Radio, December 14, 2020.* https://www.npr.org/2020/12/14/945056176/as-hospitals-fear-being-overwhelmed-by-covid-19-do-the-disabled-get-the-same-acc

assets to community readiness and resilience. When we all work together to help persons with disabilities with their health, safety, dignity, and independence, it is not only good for individuals, it also optimizes community resources. Persons with disabilities are mindful of disaster related mistakes of the past, especially those that have disproportionately impacted them and older persons. Participation is key. The public sector can lead but that leadership alone is not enough to save lives. The focus needs to be placed on ensuring that when it comes to emergencies and disasters, as well as every other aspect of community and city life, the stance of "nothing about us without us" is applied.

What we know though is that the COVID-19 pandemic won't be the last crisis of this scale. There is therefore a strong need to focus on future-proofing cities so we are better able to protect and assist people in the future, especially those most at risk. We must address issues such as the stigma around persons with disabilities as vulnerable—how will this play out in a future crisis? And how can greater inclusion of persons with disabilities in planning increase readiness and resilience?

Persons with disabilities hold a privileged vantage point in understanding and dealing with crises. They are masters of problem solving and are a special asset to be deployed and empowered. Containment measures such as social distancing are in some cases impractical or even impossible to comply with for persons with disabilities or older persons who may rely on assistance and support for the fulfillment of their daily needs.

It is therefore necessary that measures be taken to help protect the rights and livelihoods of persons with disabilities and older persons living in urban areas during emergencies or pandemics. Five of the key areas across which this needs to occur are:

- **Advocacy** to mainstream disability inclusion into all aspects of urban planning, especially in regard to climate change, public health, digital transformation, and migration.
- **Networking** to create an ecosystem approach that empowers agencies to learn and share what works. Networks encourage greater coordination between cities and stakeholders and break siloed thinking.
- **Capacity building** to strengthen people's understanding, skills, and abilities to respond to the emerging threats and shape the transformation agenda within their city. All stakeholders including local governments, industry, and civil society organizations could benefit

from widespread learning and training programs on accessibility and inclusion. These training programs should include data, monitoring, and evaluation metrics to better plan and implement effective, sustainable, and inclusive policies and programs.
- **Technical assistance** to ensure that local governments consult and partner with outside expert groups with a track record of success. These experts should include stakeholders with lived experience and deep technical knowledge of access and inclusion.
- **Inclusion champions** within all the national and local government agencies. These are people who are empowered to advocate for and build inclusive and accessible cities. These inclusion champions should include persons with disabilities as they are able to offer invaluable perspectives, know-how, resources, and expertise that has a genuine sense of clarity and purpose.

The points above should be understood as fundamental to building inclusion by design. Any governance or transformation plan in a city should center inclusion as a strategic and operational priority across all agencies. Although these insights emerged through pandemic response and recovery they were present throughout the US agencies in different ways.[18] It is evident that they in fact will also become foundational pillars of the new normal. The new normal will give civic leaders and city officials a new sense of purpose, unlock new expertise, and generate a greater level of pride through achieving better outcomes and enabling greater ownership by all stakeholders.

What Is the New Normal?

The normal wasn't normal. The normal wasn't good. We don't want to go back to that. It's revealing so much about the vulnerabilities and problems in our system. (Marina Gorbis, Executive Director, Palo Alto's Institute for the Future)

The face of the planet is changing as the cities we live in change around us. Public spaces are being redefined and reimagined. Streets are being reclaimed from cars and unused public land is being repurposed for

---

[18] For example the Americans with Disabilities Act of 1990 required all entities receiving federal funds to write an ADA transition plan, and assign an ADA coordinator to ensure barriers were identified and removed.

recreational use. But many of the changes occurring within cities continue to be problematic such as rapidly rising costs of living (including energy, transportation, food, and basic services). In addition, the pandemic saw an acceleration of mental illness, increased levels of violence, especially gender-based violence and violence against persons with disabilities, as well as an acceleration of inequality. When inequality persists, it stratifies societies for generations to come (Figs. 4.1 and 4.2).

In the case of humanitarian emergencies such as the war in Ukraine or the impacts of health pandemics, crises tend to amplify what we already know. And persons with disabilities are among those at greatest risk.[19] For example in Chicago, 35 percent of persons with disabilities live below the

Fig. 4.1 Stevenson Square, Manchester, UK. Visual description: Diners eating at picnic tables placed in the street during the temporary "pedestrianization" of Stevenson Square to allow for more social distancing during the COVID-19 pandemic. (Source: David Dixon, April 13, 2021)

[19] See the "My Disability Justice Series" piece on humanitarian responses source, www.pinedafoundation.org and Doha Debates, My Disability Justice.

Fig. 4.2 St. Mark's Place, New York City. Visual description: Outdoor diners enjoy their meals in temporary shelters designed to allow restaurant-goers to eat outside while sheltered from the elements. These structures occupy part of the roadway, demonstrating how cities can reimagine street design for pedestrians. (Image credit: Eden, Janine and Jim, https://commons.wikimedia.org/wiki/File:Dining_on_St._Marks_Place_(50295553313).jpg)

poverty line, compared to 12 percent of those without disabilities. When a crisis occurs, the already fragile systems fray under increased pressure, as was seen with issues of availability of Personal Protective Equipment (PPE) in many cities and countries. Other highly visible impacts witnessed around the world during the COVID-19 pandemic included loss of access to housing and transportation options being reduced or completely cut off. There are also human rights issues at stake, where the rights of persons with disabilities are infringed upon in relation to communication access and education rights when schools are closed. The impact of social distancing was also exacerbated for persons with disabilities who are often interdependent on others.

However, there have been positive impacts too. Cities like Amsterdam, Abu Dhabi, Bogota, Barcelona, and others have adapted to new realities by advocating and improving technologies and norms that were already favored by many persons with disabilities. This included the deployment of fully captioned virtual meetings, flexible work arrangements, grocery and food deliveries, home delivered meals, universal basic income trials, telemedicine, and a renewed interest in accessible design (e.g., via touchless fare gates and automatic door openings to help mitigate virus transmission). New relationships were forged between NGOs and government entities and disability and non-disability human service organizations working more closely together toward common goals. And new ways of communicating with communities were implemented that established new and more effective long-term processes and strategies.

Other trends evident during the pandemic included land use changes. Mixed-use real estate developments that combine residences, offices, hotels, and shops have previously had success in regenerating surrounding urban districts. COVID-19, however, created challenges for conventional operations of shops and restaurants, which in turn created difficulties for mixed-use developments. Adhering to social distancing may lead to a significant increase in car usage, reversing declines in the demand for automobile travel with long-term negative environmental repercussions. Building back better, cities must recognize the ethical imperative for a fairer distribution of urban amenities. This includes more accessible space, more space allocated to bikes and pedestrians, and more green spaces.

When it comes to deciding what we want the new normal to look like, we must seize the opportunity to rebuild our cities post-COVID so that their citizens and institutions are resilient to future shocks. Changes to working habits to favor remote working can be harnessed to make remote working an accessibility tool. Similarly, greater use of grocery and food deliveries can broaden and make permanent accessible services and infrastructure to assist persons with disabilities or older persons to have greater access to the goods and services they require. Changes to the use of outdoor space such as restaurant and outdoor dining areas can be used to rethink the amount of land prioritized for cars, turning inner city roads and carparks into car-free public or commercial spaces used to boost recreational or financial opportunities. These types of approaches allow us to take the opportunity to use changes that are occurring to alter the course of the greater physical and digital transformations already underway in our cities.

Putting the New Normal into Practice

Persons with disabilities and older persons make up more than a quarter of the world's population. The COVID-19 pandemic, climate change, migration, war, and humanitarian emergencies all pose direct threats to human rights and it is evident that responses and strategies put in place to deal with recent emergencies of this kind too often fail to achieve their intended outcomes.

The compounding nature of these crises places additional focus on the role of city leaders and local governments, who are responsible for the implementation of new guidelines, processes, and norms. Unless they can deploy new capabilities and generate new insights they will be condemned to the status quo. And unless we can measure what matters most (and understand the data we need), we will continue to create systems and processes that miss the mark on access and inclusion.

In this chapter, we discussed how cities have the potential to accelerate radical inclusion, by shaping the way citizens fulfill their potential. Below is a list of strategies and measures that can be taken by local governments to ensure a radically inclusive approach is used to design policies, services, and cities themselves. These measures should aim to:

- Promote inclusion and accessibility strategies that are a cross-cutting theme in urban governance and management.
- Enhance the training and continuous learning of city officials through specialized communities of practice and the exchange of knowledge and best practices between cities.
- Ensure that all urban transformation plans and policies are disability-inclusive, including through consultation and partnerships with persons with disabilities.
- Advance climate change responses that are participatory and inclusive of people with disabilities and that center on social resilience and equity.
- Prepare and disseminate targeted communications addressing necessary social responses to crises or emerging issues. These must include providing the community and vulnerable groups with actionable information so they can continue to make informed decisions.
- Deliver public information in accessible formats—with public communication messaging that is bias-free and respectful of all population groups, including persons with disabilities.

- Continue to build on commitments for persons with disabilities in education, digital development, data collection, transportation, and social protection.
- Promote inclusive technologies, the deployment of broadband for underserved communities, and the provision of community-based training and upskilling programs.
- Provide continued access to all goods and services, including disability-specific support services, necessary for safeguarding the wellbeing of persons with disabilities in all emergency response situations.

In conclusion, it is clear that the rapid pace of urbanization and increasing number of people living in cities has significant consequences for the health, safety, and accessibility of our urban environments. Poor urban planning can lead to inequality and exclusion, depriving certain groups of their capabilities and depriving them of their full potential as human beings. However, cities also have the potential to accelerate radical inclusion by unlocking human agency and shaping human flourishing. In the next chapter, we will explore how we can both make and measure progress in creating radically inclusive cities that provide opportunities and promote justice for all inhabitants.

Callout Box—News Article

RampMyCity, a startup making cities more able for the disabled
Source: The Hindu

Consider This RampMyCity is an accessibility startup looking to make inclusivity go beyond just infrastructural change. Started in 2018 as a simple appeal to get restaurants accessible for wheelchair users, RampMyCity now has made mainstream places of public usage like workplaces, residential societies, schools, colleges, public parks, police stations, ATMs, supermarkets, places of sports and leisure, eateries, hotels, and government buildings accessible by providing simple infrastructural solutions that carry a massive societal impact. RampMyCity also drives inclusivity by conducting sessions where hands-on training and awareness programs are given to employees and staff of various organisations to help progress attitudes, behaviors, and thought processes around persons with a disability.

The success of startups like RampMyCity, highlight the importance of expanding the solutions to accessibility and inclusion beyond government to include the capabilities and capacity of individuals and private organizations. This is especially the case in developing countries where access to public funding or public led initiatives on accessibility can be lacking. By helping to provide infrastructure solutions and conducting sessions to sensitize and train employees on disability inclusion, startups such as RampMyCity are helping to create more inclusive environments that allow greater numbers of people to access mainstream places of public usage and have equal opportunities to participate in social, cultural, recreational, and economic activities. This not only benefits persons with disabilities, but also helps to promote a more inclusive and equal society as a whole.

References

Anderson, J., Rainie, L., & Vogels, E. A. (2021, February 18). Experts say the "new normal" in 2025 will be far more tech-driven, presenting more big challenges. *PEW Research Center.* https://www.pewresearch.org/internet/2021/02/18/experts-say-the-new-normal-in-2025-will-be-far-more-tech-driven-presenting-more-big-challenges/

Armendaris, F. (2015). *World Inclusive Cities Approach Paper* (No. AUS8539). World Bank Group. https://documents1.worldbank.org/curated/en/402451468169453117/pdf/AUS8539-REVISED-WP-P148654-PUBLIC-Box393236B-Inclusive-Cities-Approach-Paper-w-Annexes-final.pdf

CBM. (n.d.). *The Inclusion Imperative: Towards Disability-inclusive and Accessible Urban Development.* Disability Inclusive and Accessible Urban Development Network. https://www.cbm.org/fileadmin/user_upload/Publications/The-Inclusion-Imperative-Towards-Disability-Inclusive-and-Accessible-Urb....pdf

Chen, B., & McNamara, D. M. (2020). Disability discrimination, medical rationing and COVID-19. *Asian Bioethics Review, 12*(4), 511–518. https://www.ncbi.nlm.nih.gov/pmc/articles/PMC7471485/

Chen, Z. (2019). Grand Challenges in Construction Management. *Frontiers in Built Environment, 5.* https://doi.org/10.3389/fbuil.2019.00031

Frey, W. H. (2021). Pandemic population change across metro America: Accelerated migration, less immigration, fewer births and more deaths. *Brookings.* https://www.brookings.edu/research/pandemic-population-change-across-metro-america-accelerated-migration-less-immigration-fewer-births-and-more-deaths/

Gould, E., & Shierholtz, H. (2020, March 19). Not everybody can work from home: Black and Hispanic workers are much less likely to be able to telework. *Economic Policy Institute.* Retrieved May 17, 2023, from https://www.epi.org/blog/black-and-hispanic-workers-are-much-less-likely-to-be-able-to-work-from-home/

HABITAT III. (2015). *HABITAT III ISSUE PAPERS 1 – INCLUSIVE CITIES.* United Nations. https://uploads.habitat3.org/hb3/Habitat-III-Issue-Paper-1_Inclusive-Cities-2.0.pdf

Harris, R. (2021). *How Cities Matter.* Cambridge University Press.

Mishra, P. & Gowda, B. (2022, November 11). RampMyCity, a startup making cities more able for the disabled. *The Hindu.* https://www.thehindu.com/news/cities/bangalore/rampmycity-this-startup-making-cities-more-able-for-the-disabled/article66125754.ece

Nussbaum, M. C. (2007). Frontiers of Justice: Disability, Nationality, Species Membership. Harvard University Press. https://doi.org/10.4159/9780674041578

Pineda, V. (n.d.). Webinar 4: Age-Friendly Cities. *Combined Accessibility Blogs.*

Pineda, V. S. (2008). Enabling justice: Spatializing disability in the built environment. *Critical Planning Journal, 15,* 111–123.

Pineda, V. (2020). *Building the Inclusive City: Governance, Access, and the Urban Transformation of Dubai.* Palgrave Springer. https://link.springer.com/book/10.1007/978-3-030-32988-4

Pineda, V., & Corburn, J. (2020). Disability, urban health equity, and the Coronavirus pandemic: Promoting cities for all. *Journal of Urban Health, 97*(3), 336–341. https://doi.org/10.1007/s11524-020-00437-7

Schweik, S. M. (2010). *The Ugly Laws: Disability in public.* NYU Press.

Shapiro, J. (2020, December 14). As hospital fear being overwhelmed by COVID-19, do the disabled get the same access? *National Public Radio.* https://www.npr.org/2020/12/14/945056176/as-hospitals-fear-being-overwhelmed-by-covid-19-do-the-disabled-get-the-same-acc

United Nations, Department of Economic and Social Affairs, Population Division. (2018). *2018 Revision of the World Urbanization Prospects.* https://esa.un.org/unpd/wup/

Open Access This chapter is licensed under the terms of the Creative Commons Attribution 4.0 International License (http://creativecommons.org/licenses/by/4.0/), which permits use, sharing, adaptation, distribution and reproduction in any medium or format, as long as you give appropriate credit to the original author(s) and the source, provide a link to the Creative Commons licence and indicate if changes were made.

The images or other third party material in this chapter are included in the chapter's Creative Commons licence, unless indicated otherwise in a credit line to the material. If material is not included in the chapter's Creative Commons licence and your intended use is not permitted by statutory regulation or exceeds the permitted use, you will need to obtain permission directly from the copyright holder.

CHAPTER 5

Making and Measuring Progress in Radically Inclusive Cities

Abstract The cities of Dubai and Abu Dhabi can serve as useful examples of the journey cities can undertake toward radical inclusion for persons with disabilities in the context of rapid urbanization. The actions of these cities over previous decades provide examples of practical approaches to building more inclusion and belonging by design. The management, governance, and strategies they undertook demonstrate how consistent and measurable progress toward inclusion, equity, and accessibility can be effectively designed and executed. Two frameworks, the DisCo Policy Framework and the Iceberg of Inequality Model, can be used to complement these city-based case studies. The DisCo Policy Framework is a tool for evaluating inclusive urban development and has five interrelated criteria for assessment. The Iceberg of Inequality Model shows the hierarchical structure of primary rights and capabilities. These tools can be used to benchmark progress toward radical inclusion and form part of a multidimensional and cross-sectional toolkit for key stakeholders to undo decades old errors and omissions in broad based planning, policy, and design. The UN Habitat III Conference also highlighted six key areas for advancing equity, access, and inclusion in cities as well as the need for political commitment to inclusive urbanization.

Keywords DisCo policy framework • Iceberg of inequality model • Legislative measures • Executive and budgetary support • Administrative and coordinating capacity • Basic functionings • Basic freedoms • Age-friendly cities

© The Author(s) 2024
V. S. Pineda, *Inclusion and Belonging in Cities of Tomorrow*,
https://doi.org/10.1007/978-981-99-3856-8_5

Once we have the universal goal it doesn't mean therefore treat everybody the same. It's not saying treat everyone the same because everybody's not in the same situation. People need to be treated differently. This is different from equity, at least equity in the narrow sense. Because equity oftentimes normalizes what the dominant group has and says let's close the disparity but it's assuming that when we close the disparity we're basically done. What if the dominant group doesn't have what they need either? (john powell[1], Director, Institute on Othering and Belonging, University of California, Berkeley)

Dubai is a city of dreams and extremes, it's a city of diverse peoples, of diverse neighborhoods, each with its own unique character and charm. As a Fulbright-Hays scholar I had the chance to get to know every part of this city. It was my job. In 2009, I was a visiting fellow at the Mohammed bin Rashid School of Government (at the time the Dubai School of Government). I assessed access barriers all over From the Palm Island to the bustling streets of Deira to the sandy beaches of Jumeirah, even at that time there was something for everyone in this metropolis, but not if you had a disability.

Since those early years Dubai has transformed into one of the world's most accessible and inclusive cities. This was not an accident. Diversity and inclusion were prioritized and built by design. In 2014, My colleague Dr. Sandra Willis and I co-authored the Dubai Disability Strategy, marking a vital moment in shaping the future growth of the city to be more inclusive and accessible to all.

Now as I explore the various neighborhoods of Dubai, I am struck by the progress that has been made toward creating a radically inclusive city. From the accessible public transportation and buildings to the welcoming airport staff, and inclusive community spaces, there are many examples of how the city is working to create a place that truly belongs to all. I recognize that there is still work to be done. No city is perfect, and every city is a living and evolving human creation, shaped by the experiences and expectations of its inhabitants. The leadership there recognizes that inclusivity is not a binary, but a journey with different experiences and

---

[1] John Powell has purposefully chosen to display his name in lowercase letters. In keeping with other African American scholars like bell hooks, to note the primacy of their work and not the title or status of their given names. There are cultural, historic, and political reasons by which descendants of slaves have chosen to adopt this naming format. Learn more at the Institute for Othering and Belonging.

perspectives. It's a place where stakeholders work together to create a city that has a dynamic and complex relationship to inclusion and belonging.

This chapter illustrates that ideals are not easy or straightforward to achieve. Ideals set a directive—and it is just that, an ideal. But how do make and measure progress, especially when cities are living and evolving human creations? They are in a constant process of becoming and this journey is shaped by the experiences and expectations of their inhabitants. This is a journey with different experiences and perspectives; different winners and losers co-existing and renegotiating their social, economic, cultural, and political needs and renegotiating the relative positioning of what they value.

Even Burning Man at Black Rock City, which names radical inclusion as the first of its ten core principles, is but an experiment of radical inclusion and exclusion. For many it is simply not financially accessible for many. That cities may never become wholly radically inclusive doesn't mean we should abandon all efforts to realize radical inclusion. Rather, the process by which a city implements radically inclusive approaches is how we create sustainable, resilient, and yes, inclusive cities of tomorrow.

In this chapter, I provide some examples of how two cities in the United Arab Emirates have taken on the task of advancing radical inclusion for persons with disabilities. I next introduce two frameworks to complement the case studies we have explored to this point. The two frameworks are the DisCo Policy Framework and the Iceberg of Inequality Model, including discussion of the theories and precedents that informed their creation. These tools can be used to benchmark progress toward radical inclusion and form part of a multidimensional and cross-sectional toolkit for key stakeholders to undo decades old errors and omissions in broad based planning, policy, and design. Then, I discuss six key areas highlighted by the UN Habitat III Conference that advance equity, access, and inclusion in cities and the necessity of political commitment to inclusive urbanization. Finally, I consider what it means to be intentional through design and why radical inclusion differs entirely from efforts to simply "bolt on" accessibility.

As this section shows, efforts by the cities of Dubai and Abu Dhabi provide examples of practical approaches to building more inclusion and belonging by design. The management, governance, and strategies demonstrate how consistent and measurable progress toward inclusion, equity, and accessibility can be designed and executed.

Some questions arise at this point: How can insights and experiences from different cities be concretely replicated and scaled? How can we measure and evaluate progress on radical inclusion? What are the common short falls on the radical inclusion roadmap? And how can avoiding them be systematized? Answering these questions allows us to design governance systems and institutional approaches that build belonging by design. In the next sections we will provide some tools to help advance this aim.

THE DisCo POLICY FRAMEWORK

The DisCo Urban Policy assessment framework is a tool that can help city managers and other urban stakeholders assess the inclusivity and resilience of their urban development efforts. It was developed in 2010 to provide a structured approach to data collection and to align local efforts with international normative frameworks. The framework includes five interrelated criteria, or pillars, for evaluating inclusive urban development: legislative measures, executive and budgetary support, administrative and coordinating capacity, participation of targeted groups, and attitudes toward targeted groups. By using the DisCo framework, stakeholders can identify the key areas a project is addressing and member states or city leaders can conduct rapid assessments at the neighborhood, city, or national level.

Complex socio-economic and inclusivity issues are rooted in decades long urban planning failures or complete omissions. As you read the following criteria, consider how you could conduct a rapid assessment of a policy issue at the scale of your neighborhood, city, state, or nation. Doing so could help you find gaps and identify potential solutions to existing shortcomings.

Pillar 1: Legislative Measures (Laws and Norms)

The first pillar is informed by the tradition of critical legal theory. Authority, politics, immutability, and neutrality are all natural products of a legal order. Critical legal theory also questions the epistemologies and genealogies of intellectual history that dominate our ways of understanding both the world and legality. Norms are shortcuts for behavior because of their role in informing reasoning processes (Kratochwil 1991).[2] Laws are

---

[2] Kratochwil, F.V., (1991). Rules, norms, and decisions: On the conditions of practical and legal reasoning in international relations and domestic affairs. *Cambridge University Press.*

informed by these norms, because norms simplify choices for actors with non-identical preferences.

When it comes to the development of policy, it is a contentious, political process and relies on the importance of persuasion. Policy arguments are selective, both shaping and shaped by regimes of power, which includes beliefs, attitudes, and values. Social constructs play a primary role in policy creation. Social constructions can be defined as the (typically negative and unrealistic) pre-existing notions, assumptions, stereotypes, associations, and representations of groups, populations, and histories. These social constructions tend to be the product of dominant regimes of truth, or the cultural spirit of the times, circulated by discourses, social structures, practices, and the media. Ultimately, these constructs manifest themselves throughout all sectors of society, including policy and law. Not only do these constructs impact the material welfare of target groups, but they also influence their social reputations, political attitudes, and participation patterns. Therefore groups lying at the margins of society (via exclusionary policy practices due to pre-existing social constructs) are often deemed unworthy of political inclusion and participation in policy (Baumgartner et al. 2018).[3]

It is also important to recognize the importance of language, both in policy and as a part of common usage in a given time. This is because language doesn't simply mirror the world, it also has the power to profoundly shape our view of it in the first place (Forester 1993).[4] The development of policy is a contentious, political process and relies on the importance of persuasion. Policy arguments are selective, both shaping and shaped by regimes of power, which includes beliefs, attitudes, and values. Social constructs play a primary role in policy creation. Social constructions can be defined as the (typically negative and unrealistic) pre-existing notions, assumptions, stereotypes, associations, and representations of groups, populations, and histories. These social constructions tend to be the product of dominant regimes of truth, or the cultural spirit of the times, circulated by discourses, social structures, practices, and the media. Ultimately, these constructs manifest themselves throughout all sectors of society, including policy and law. Not only do these constructs "impact the mate-

---

[3] Baumgartner, F. R. Jones, B.D. and Mortensen, P.B. (2018). Punctuated equilibrium theory: Explaining stability and change in public policymaking. *Theories of the policy process (2018): 55–101.*

[4] Forester, J. (1993) Critical theory, public policy, and planning practice. *SUNY Press.*

rial welfare of target groups [in policy practices] but [they] also influence their social reputations, political attitudes, and participation patterns." Therefore groups lying at the margins of society (via exclusionary policy practices due to pre-existing social constructs) are typically deemed unworthy of political inclusion and participation in policy (Baumgartner et al. 2018).[5]

It is also important to recognize the importance of language, both in policy and as a part of common usage in a given time. This is because language doesn't simply mirror the world, it also has the power to profoundly shape our view of it in the first place (Forester 1993).[6] Normative and deliberate language plays a vital role in the production of inclusive and equitable laws. This points to the importance of rethinking how norms, discourses, and the political-sociology of knowledge informs the possibilities of action and knowing within the legal system what is necessary to advance aspirations for inclusive law.

Pillar 2: Executive and Budgetary Support

Political cultures shape preferences around the organization of social activity and therefore shape resource allocation within prevailing structures. Therefore resource allocation in any given context epitomizes the prevailing structures and modes of power of the time.

The realities of resource scarcity necessitate the prioritization of political and collective actions, meaning that budgets become more than just mechanisms for allocating resources or the pursuit of efficiency, they also inevitably reflect social values. Therefore, the ways in which budgets are allocated tend to serve as a lens to examine dominant cultural and ideological imaginaries (the zeitgeist). These are then manifested through political choices and the processes that shape social life (Wildavsky 1986).[7]

Understanding the allocation and distribution of power and wealth can contribute to fostering more equitable and inclusive outcomes for persons with disabilities and other marginalized groups (Baumgartner et al.

---

[5] See footnote 3.
[6] *Ibid.* Forester, J. (1993).
[7] Wildavsky, A. B. (1986) Budgeting: a comparative theory of the budgeting process. *Transaction Publishers.*

2018).[8] Budgets can therefore be seen as one mechanism for constructing and maintaining social values and budget analysis allows for the examination of cultural norms. In this way, political cultures and the social values of the zeitgeist, born out through the ways in which budgets are allocated, become critical in the development of an inclusive society that considers the needs of disabled individuals.

Pillar 3: Administrative and Coordinating Capacity

The twenty-first century has brought turbulent changes, brought about by globalization and hyper-competition trends paired with a weakening of global governance. The end result of this is an urgent need to internationally strengthen administrative capacities. Local agencies often lack the institutional capacity or human resources necessary to implement substantive changes.

Strengthening the public sector and its services should be done externally via legislation and a reinforcing of the appropriate role for governments as the guardians of society in domestic and international affairs. It also needs to involve engaging citizens, community organizations, and other organizational institutions in governance and administration. Transparency plays a key role in this process, as it supports the emphasis placed on increasing citizen participation, trust, and confidence in governmental practices (Farazmand 2009).[9]

Governments should look to conduct stakeholder mapping to better understand possible deficits in administrative and coordinating capacity and determine if the responsible parties are effectively working across sectors and scales. By looking closely at this pillar, program fragmentation and overlap can be avoided.

Pillar 4: Participation of the Targeted Group

Participation and representation processes are crucial to inclusive decision-making in urban planning processes. In addition to various other benefits

---

[8] Baumgartner, F. R., Jones, B. D. and Mortensen, P. B. (2018). Punctuated equilibrium theory: Explaining stability and change in public policymaking. *Theories of the policy process (2018): 55–101.*

[9] Farazmand, A. (2009). Building administrative capacity for the age of rapid globalization: A modest prescription for the twenty-first century. *Public Administration Review 69.6 (2009): 1007–1020.*

such as the decentralization of interests and more innovative decisions, they provide a more nuanced and cautious cultural translation of inclusive decision-making within domestic and international settings. This helps ensure the unified implementation of decisions with a minimization of unintended consequences via cultural barriers.

Methods for planning should emphasize the interaction with and creation of public consultation techniques that increase public support and participatory input. All these recommendations for citizen participation in planning purposes are crucial when we consider the existence of unequal power dynamics. Participatory decision-making is important for power equalization in the public sector. Systemic exclusion of populations whose power lies in the margins of society are those whose input is most crucial to planning processes.

There should be a consensual understanding between planning agencies and the general public on what constitutes "citizen participation," how the concept is put into practice, what resources are required, and what the various decision-making responsibilities will entail. This form of collaborative planning minimizes the room for error in the conceptualization of the citizenry's desires and the actions of planning agencies (Fagence 1977).[10]

To these ends, governments should report on the level of participation of targeted beneficiaries in urban development. They should also report on the number of persons with disabilities in leadership positions, as well as the quality and types of engagements between local governments and disabled persons organization.

Pillar 5: Attitudes Toward the Targeted Group

Attitudes and beliefs are extremely important to disability policy and inclusion because of the ways in which they directly and indirectly influence courses of social action. There are three factors that interchangeably influence attitudes: affect, beliefs, and behavior. Affect is the moment of initial impact and feeling that people experience given any set encounters or events. Beliefs are mental shortcuts for associating people or events with a given characteristic. Behaviors are defined as the actions of an individual. These factors reciprocally affect and are affected by attitudes, with the key point here being that attitudes are not set in stone. Attitudes and beliefs

---

[10] Fagence, M. (2014). Citizen Participation in Planning (Vol. 19). *Elsevier.*

shift with respect to an individual's perception of their environments. However, attitudes and beliefs are also a product of the discourses and worldviews circulated within those environments; thus, people's beliefs both shape and are shaped by the socio-cultural context in which they are embedded (Albarracin et al. 2005).[11]

Political rhetoric and cultural discourses produce negative associations to people with physical or mental disabilities by superficially assuming high dependency. This is in contrast to policies and actions aimed at empowerment. This highlights the importance of the interchanging dynamics between beliefs and attitudes about marginalized groups. By being inclusive in policy processes, we can contribute to the rethinking of pre-existing attitudes and beliefs about marginalized populations.

Governments and cities should report on their efforts to promote and monitor awareness raising efforts. This includes reporting on the metrics used to assess communication and outreach initiatives (via both social media and traditional media). In addition, it is important to continuously study the prevalence of biases and negative attitudes toward persons with disabilities, which inhibits further progress from being made.

When conducting data collection efforts, these must be strong, multi-stakeholder efforts that promote sustained collaboration, information sharing, and knowledge exchange between all disability and development actors. Strong coordination of data collection efforts helps ensure that policies and programs actually generate the desired changes.

Five Pillars of DisCo Policy Framework

1. Legislative Measures
2. Executive and Budgetary Support
3. Administrative and Coordinating Capacity
4. Participation of Targeted Group
5. Attitudes Toward Targeted Group

[11] Zanna, D. A. M. P., Johnson, B. T., & Kumkale, G. T. (2005). Attitudes: Introduction and Scope. *The Handbook of Attitudes*, 3–20.

A primary goal in the development of the DisCo framework was to establish a conversation among the divergent fields of inquiry, knowledge, and expertise, by gathering the data necessary to create a starting point that stakeholders could then build upon. Robust, multi-stakeholder platforms that support information sharing and sustained collaboration between all disability and development actors can greatly facilitate the accessibility and inclusion of international cooperation programs, ultimately resulting in more inclusive cities.

THE ICEBERG OF INEQUALITY

The Iceberg of Inequality model helps to highlight the primary rights in a hierarchical form.

The basic functionings provide a baseline from which to build and expand capabilities through increasing basic freedoms.

Basic functionings are differentiated from basic freedoms in the following ways:

1. Basic functionings are understood as primary needs and are thus fundamental to the enjoyment of all of an individual's rights.
2. Basic freedoms are necessary to expand basic functionings into capabilities, which are in themselves the goal of development. Basic freedoms allow for capabilities and functionings to be converted into social value. They also allow persons with disabilities to live the type of life they "have reason to value" (Sen 1999).[12]

Capabilities can also be presented as a function of an individual's basic functionings (BFn) and basic freedoms (BFr):

Capabilities = $f(\text{BFn}+\text{BFr})$

The pillars can be used to display multiple dimensions of exclusion and benchmark inclusion and they can do so across the various dimensions through the Iceberg of Inequality (Fig. 5.1).

---

[12] Sen, A. (1999) Commodities and capabilities. *OUP Catalogue*.

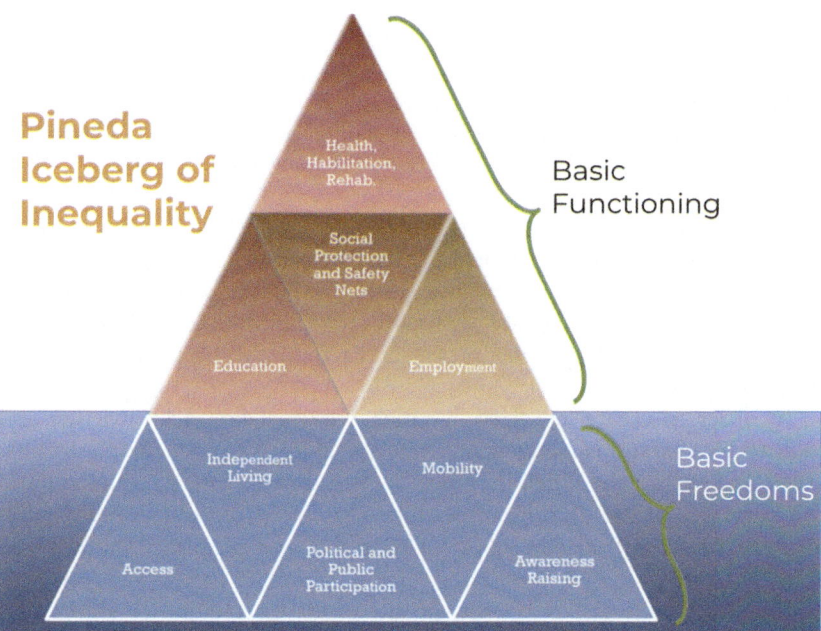

Fig. 5.1 The Pineda Iceberg of Inequality. This diagram shows an "iceberg" or triangle where the first layer (under the water) lists basic freedoms: Access, Independent Living, Political and Public Participation, Mobility, and Awareness Raising. The second layer, above the water, is Basic Functioning and shows Education, Social Protection and Safety Nets, Employment, and at the top: Health, Habilitation, Rehabilitation

The Iceberg of Inequality is a conceptual model for understanding the basic policy areas or sectors that need to come together to create systemic and holistic change. These factors support a holistic approach, one that further calibrates a set of agencies and responsible parties to align around the principles of radical inclusion. How might we operationalize radical inclusion? What other initiatives exist that have the potential to transform systems and create new models for governance and models for building belonging by design? Finally, what can we learn from these existing models and efforts?

Age-Friendly Cities

Active aging means to have an active and healthy life, to continue to enjoy, learn, make decisions, contribute and connect as we age. (Shu-Ti Chiou, Global Vice-President for Capacity Building, Education and Training, International Union for Health Promotion & Education)

The World Health Organization describes age-friendly cities as inclusive and accessible urban environments that promote active aging. Age-friendly cities promote active aging through a whole-of-government and whole-of-society ecological approach to developing comprehensive enabling policies, built environments, and activities to support active aging for all.

In order to create age-friendly cities, we must first acknowledge and look to understand how ageism affects the ability of older people to fully enjoy and utilize the cities they live in. It's also necessary to understand the enormity of the demographic shifts that are occurring in many cities and countries around the world. The global age profile is shifting and shifting rapidly.

In 2019, the population over the age of 60 represented 1 billion people, or around 13 percent of the global population. Of those 1 billion, 46 percent are defined as having one or more disabilities. There is therefore a clear and important overlap between older people and those with a disability. Today, 58 percent of people over 60 live in Asia and the Pacific region.

In 2030, the population over 60 will rise to 1.4 billion or 17 percent of the projected global population. By 2050, it will be 2.1 billion or 21 percent of the population. With this increase in the proportion of the population over the age of 60 will come a corresponding increase in the proportion of people who live with a disability.

There are many similarities in the stigmas that older persons and persons with a disability face every day. We have all encountered stigmatism to some extent, whether we have a disability, or whether we are older or younger. It is a form of discrimination, which is simply an act by those who are ignoring and sometimes empowered to prevent people from being able to exercise their human rights. Especially for older persons and those with a disability, stigma can cause people to be treated differently to the extent that it often drives people to hide illness to avoid discrimination. It can also lead to older people being actively targeted and preyed upon with misinformation or scams.

Age-Accessible Transportation

We need age-accessible transportation so older persons as well as disabled persons can easily travel. This has important wider implications, allowing them to connect with the whole city. This involves ensuring:

- Public transportation costs are consistent, clearly displayed, and affordable.
- Vehicles are clean, well-maintained, accessible, not overcrowded, and have priority seating that is respected.
- Specialized transportation is available for disabled people.
- A voluntary transport service is available where public transportation is too limited.
- Traffic signs and intersections are clearly visible and well-placed.

To develop age-friendly cities with appropriate transportation, the first step is to engage political leaders at national and local levels. The second step is to build an intersectional community, not only leaders but experts joining the government on these types of initiatives. It's also important to put older persons' perspectives at the center of the decision-making process. This includes looking at their needs and demands, identifying weaknesses in systems, and helping to develop comprehensive communications channels. Outreach is required to connect with people living alone who are older or disabled.

The age-friendly city movement provides the additional benefit of strengthening societal resilience against the COVID-19 outbreak and similar pandemics. This is because citizens are engaged and communications channels are already in place to connect with isolated or potentially vulnerable people.

The Impact and Legacy of a New Urban Agenda

As an urban planner with lived experience of disability, I understood that the existing urban policies neglected the voices and perspectives of many groups, particularly persons with disabilities and older persons. By 2015, the United Nations Conference on Housing and Sustainable Urban Development was already a few years into its global stakeholder engagements. Manuel Rodas, the Mayor of Quito, Ecuador and a wheelchair user, Lenin Morena, the Vice-President at the time would host the conference and unite the world around principles that would shape the future of cities.[13] In May of 2016, six months before the conference, I received an email from a high-level UN Official with a draft of the New Urban Agenda, which was the proposed outcome document of the conference. Within the 150 paragraphs of this international agreement they noted that persons with disabilities were only referenced once, (and that was simply within an extensive list of many other marginalized groups). What struck me was that this specific paragraph was not intentional or specific about what types of interventions, standards, approaches, or protections should be advanced.

To respond to this oversight, World Enabled, CBM, and the World Blind Union mobilized a global campaign with over 180 individuals and organizations to advocate for a more robust engagement with the disability community. The Global Network for Disability Inclusive and Accessible Urban Development (DIAUD) secured 15 substantive references to persons with disabilities in the final document.[14] It was a monumental achievement to reverse course and force other national governments to reconsider their endorsement of the penultimate draft. At the convening and final assembly, there were more than 30 thousand people who participated. More than 2000 representatives of local and regional governments received accreditation. This event convened one of the widest ranges of stakeholders ever assembled by the UN system.[15]

These groups came together with hundreds of local and national governments, research institutions, civil society networks, and grassroots organizations to shape the principles that will shape our urban future. In full force was our group of 30 DIAUD delegates representing persons with disabilities from all over the world. At the conclusion of these negotiations, the New Urban Agenda was released, a UN declaration signed by

---

[13] Habitat III also highlighted the voices of two senior political leaders, the Vice Presidents of Ecuador (Lenin Moreno) and Argentina (Gabriela Michetti) who both participated and spoke on stage. What was remarkable was that these two senior leaders were also wheelchair users. Vice President Moreno representing the host country was personally engaged with the conference planning and oversaw one the strongest participations of civil society, stakeholders, and local authorities in the history of the United Nations. See Habitat III Legacy Website.

[14] As one of the negotiators in the room with representatives of the EU, United States, Russia, Japan, Ecuador, Malaysia, South Africa, and other countries.

[15] Over 30,000 people from 167 countries participated at the Conference.

167 nations, which laid out a 20-year roadmap for sustainable urban development.[16]

The Habitat III Issue Papers[17] highlighted six areas that engaged ten policy units: Social Cohesion and Equity—Livable Cities, Urban Frameworks, Spatial Development, Urban Economy, Urban Ecology and Environment, and Urban Housing and Basic Services. Over 100 global experts collaborated to produce a total of 21 papers; however, these overwhelmingly failed to explicitly mention vital issues and themes such as Universal Design, accessibility, and disability rights. Each gap and policy unit could have been further reviewed by an access and inclusion expert, or someone with insights and understanding of urban process and planning. The following five discussion points summarize efforts made to advance equity, access, and inclusion in cities.[18]

1. **Participation and Social Innovation in Planning, Implementation, and Evaluation**

Participatory planning approaches that center the experiences and input of traditionally excluded groups are key to shaping radically inclusive cities. Decisions on where to place bus stops, for example, should be informed by the experiences of disabled people and women, who are more likely to face the consequences of inaccessible or dangerous placements.

This process allows stakeholders who hold disparate interests to work collectively to solve problems. Urban planning initiatives that help the elderly navigate the city independently may also be beneficial to individuals with disabilities, or children, who also wish to maneuver around the city independently.

---

[16] The Sustainable Development Goals and the New Urban Agenda recognize the role of cities in achieving sustainable development. However, these agendas were agreed and signed by national governments and thus implementing them at the local level requires a process of adaptation or localization. The New Urban Agenda highlights linkages between a range of areas including sustainable urbanization and job creation and livelihood opportunities and improved quality of life. It also insists on incorporation of these sectors in every urban development or renewal policy and strategy.

[17] Issue Papers can be found on the Habitat III legacy page https://habitat3.org/documents-and-archive/preparatory-documents/issue-papers/

[18] The Habitat III Issue Papers were prepared by the United Nations Task Team on Habitat III. This was a task force of UN agencies and programs that came together to work toward the elaboration of the New Urban Agenda. The Issue Papers were finalized during the UN Task Team writeshop held in New York in 2015.

2. Realizing the Rights of All to Universal Access to Physical Spaces and Basic Services

All people deserve to be able to access basic quality services without difficulty. The universal nature of this right necessitates targeted interventions to ensure that all groups and demographics have the same access to services such as affordable housing, health care (including reproductive care and mental health care), nutritious food, safe water and sanitation, education, and income security.

Approaches to guarantee these rights must be developed through participatory planning programs to ensure that no groups are left out or under-resourced. Particular attention must be placed on supporting migrant populations given the number of people migrating to cities each year (which is only expected to rise).

3. Spatial Planning for Inclusion

Forward-thinking spatial planning is critical to ensuring that cities become more inclusive, accessible, and resilient into the future. Planning initiatives to facilitate equal access to job opportunities can help lessen inequality between residential and working areas. These approaches can also ensure that new residents of urban areas have access to safe and sustainable work and a living wage. These and other approaches will help support the economic transitions facing urban environments.

4. Accountability

Transparency and effective oversight measures are necessary for reducing corruption and protecting public interests. The city of Cebu in the Philippines developed gender responsive community report cards to demonstrate the efficacy of government efforts and to otherwise monitor performance. These report cards have helped the city respond to the particular needs of women and develop initiatives to prevent and respond to gender-based violence.

Open access to government databases can provide the public with information on development plans, disaster risks and evacuation information, budgeting, and other areas of interest. These efforts promote decision-making that is publicly informed and supported and allows for partnerships with and input from community organizations such as disability rights organizations (DPOs).

5. **Understanding the Roles of National and Local Government in Generating Inclusive Urbanization**

Partnerships between local and national governments and among local governments can allow for widespread targeted interventions to address common problems throughout a region. Efforts to promote sustainable and inclusive urban growth must be a key priority to both local and national governments and municipalities should work together to address discrepancies between policy approaches.

Specifically, national policies can hinder or enable local governments in their efforts to generate inclusive environments such as when national immigration enforcement programs clash with so-called "sanctuary cities."

RADICALLY INCLUSIVE CITIES IN PRACTICE

Cities that are radically inclusive effectively monitor, measure, and evaluate progress on radical inclusion in urban governance. These cities have strong accountability mechanisms paired with capable leadership. They develop core capabilities that allow them to align policies with practical, measurable actions. To support this, radically inclusive cities implement data, monitoring, and evaluation mechanisms across a variety of interconnected agencies and task forces. Finally, they engage in continuous learning and ensure that a cross-cutting, radically inclusive approach is being applied to unlock existing knowledge and underutilized resources. Below we dive deeper into how to do this and how city leaders and other urban stakeholders can take action.

Adopt Standards to Advance Universal Accessibility in the Built Environment

Encourage Design Standards Appropriate to the Community Context
Design standards are specific criteria and requirements that dictate the form, function, and appearance of development in a physical or digital space. These standards can be used to improve accessibility and protect the function and esthetic appeal of a community or neighborhood. Some

examples of design standards include guidelines for building placement, building massing and materials, and the location and appearance of elements such as landscaping, signage, and street furniture. It is important for these standards to consider accessibility for persons with disabilities, such as by including accessible information kiosks in key public buildings or designing busy entrance ways with mobility impaired people in mind. Accessible design standards can encourage development that is compatible with the community context and enhances a sense of place. While a comprehensive city-wide master plan may not specify detailed accessibility standards, it can establish the direction and objectives that these standards should aim to achieve, such as ensuring that new development meets certain accessibility requirements.

Provide Accessible and Smart Public Facilities and Spaces
Public facilities play an important role in every city, and they should be able to accommodate persons of all ages and abilities. Public facilities including digital spaces such as online forums, social media, websites, apps, as well as schools, parks, civic or community centers, public safety facilities, arts and cultural facilities, recreational facilities, and plazas, should be accessible to all regardless of whether they have difficulty seeing, hearing, or speaking. They should be located and designed to be safe, served by different transportation modes, and accessible to visitors with mobility impairments.

Adopt Standards to Advance Accessibility Through Integrated, Multimodal Transportation Systems

Plan for Smart and Holistic Multimodal Transportation
A smart multimodal transportation system allows people to use a variety of transportation modes including walking, biking, and other mobility devices (e.g., wheelchairs) and access the transit services and information digitally where possible. Such a system reduces dependence on automobiles, offers more choice, and encourages more active forms of personal transportation. This leads to improved health outcomes and increases the mobility of those who are unable or unwilling to drive. Fewer cars on the road also translate to reduced air pollution and greenhouse gas emissions with associated health and environmental benefits.

Plan for Transit-Oriented Development
Transit-oriented development (TOD) is characterized by a concentration of higher density mixed use development around transit stations and along transit lines to encourage public transit use and pedestrian activity. TOD allows communities to focus on new residential and commercial development in areas that are well-connected to public transit. This enables residents to more easily use transit services, which can reduce vehicle-miles traveled and fossil fuels consumed and associated reductions in pollution and greenhouse gas emissions. It can also reduce the need for personal automobile ownership, resulting in a decreased need for parking spaces and other automobile-oriented infrastructure.

Provide Complete Streets Serving Multiple Functions
Complete streets are designed and operated with all users in mind—including motorists, pedestrians, bicyclists, and public transit riders (where applicable) of all ages and abilities—to support an accessible and affordable multimodal transportation system. A complete street network is one that safely and conveniently accommodates all users and desired functions, though this does not mean that all modes or functions will be equally prioritized on any given street segment. Streets that serve multiple functions can accommodate travel, social interaction, and commerce to provide for more vibrant neighborhoods and more livable communities.

Adopt Standards to Integrate Land Use, Climate Resilience, Historic Preservation With Social Inclusion

Plan for Mixed Land-Use Patterns That Are Walkable and Bikeable
Mixed land-use patterns are characterized by residential and nonresidential land uses located in close proximity to one another. Incorporating safe, convenient, smart, accessible, and attractive design features (e.g., sidewalks with sensors, bike street furniture, bicycle sharing, street trees, public wi-fi), mixed land uses, and providing housing in close proximity to everyday destinations (e.g., shops, civic places, workplaces) can increase walking and biking and increase personal mobility.

Prioritize Access With Infill Development
Infill development is characterized by development or redevelopment of undeveloped or underutilized parcels of land in otherwise built-up areas.

These are usually served by or have ready access to existing infrastructure and services. Ensure all new construction incorporates national or ISO accessibility standards.

Implement Accessibility Standards into Green Building Design and Energy Conservation
A green building is characterized by design features that, if used as intended, will minimize the environmental impacts of the building over the course of its lifespan. In addition, social sustainability including principles of Universal Design should be considered in parallel to environmental impact assessment. This reduces the need to retrofit in the future and supports change of behavior that is more accepting of accessibility.

Conserve and Enhance Historic Resources
Historic resources are buildings, sites, landmarks, or districts with exceptional value or quality for illustrating or interpreting the cultural heritage of a city. It is important to address digital accessibility in accessing information, as well as ensuring the conservation and enhancement efforts improve accessibility as much as possible.

CASE STUDY FROM THE UNITED ARAB EMIRATES

Dubai and Abu Dhabi, located in the United Arab Emirates, are cities that have undergone significant transformation in the nearly 52 years since the UAE's independence in 1971. These cities, known for their iconic skylines and record-setting skyscrapers, have become global centers for business, finance, and leisure, with a focus on continuous change and development. The transformation of these cities has been driven by the vision of their leadership, which has sought to turn them into more than just regional hubs by constructing towering skyscrapers and artificial islands. Today, Dubai and Abu Dhabi are examples of cities that have successfully embraced accessibility within a framework of modernity and the principles of avant-gardism, as exemplified by their iconic architecture and inclusive and accessible features of their tourism sector, including their indoor ski slopes.

The United Arab Emirates has experienced rapid urban, infrastructural, and economic growth in recent years, with a population increase from 235,000 in 1970 to 9,991,000 in 2021. It is important to note that 90 percent of this population consists of immigrants. Among the UAE's cities, Dubai is the largest, with a population of 2.4 million. Abu Dhabi, the capital, and Dubai have developed broad city-scale agendas that engage stakeholders from the government, private sector, and communities. These agendas, which often have high levels of support, have created opportunities for collaboration and have helped to ensure the success of future city plans. Two agendas that are currently prioritized in both Dubai and Abu Dhabi are "Smart," "Happy," and "Tolerant," which aim to promote innovation, digitalization, diversity, social inclusion, and equality as key drivers for a more equitable, inclusive, and sustainable future for all.

The cities of Dubai and Abu Dhabi have made concerted efforts to align their ambitious urban development plans with the key global agendas. Equity, justice, and access in the rapidly urbanizing city-states of Dubai and Abu Dhabi shape the story of disability in the UAE, starting with the first center for children with disabilities in the 1980s to UAE's ratification of the UN Convention on the Rights of Persons with Disabilities (CRPD) in 2008, and later in 2014 when Dubai's legal, institutional, physical, and social reforms led to the passage of Dubai Law No. 2 on the Rights of Persons with Disabilities, and the launch of the Dubai Disability Strategy one year later. The Higher Committee for the Protection of the Rights of Persons with Disabilities was established to (1) oversee the implementation of the law, (2) meet the CRPD obligations and Sustainable Development Goals (SDGs) targets, and (3) establish a governance model outlining the role of private and public sectors and civil society institutions in developing practical steps to support the related legislations and laws, programmatic and policy choices, organizational values and working practices, and the mainstreaming of disability by providing quality, affordable and inclusive healthcare; education; employment and social protective services; and accessible built, digital, and transportation amenities, systems, and environments.

It was an inspired vision by the Dubai leadership to make Dubai an inclusive, barrier-free, rights-based society that promotes, protects, and ensures the self-determination of people with disabilities or, as aptly coined in October 2017 by H.H. Sheikh Mohammed bin Rashid Al Maktoum, the Vice President and Prime Minister of the UAE and ruler of Dubai, "People of Determination." Dubai serves as an ideal case study in understanding the public response to developing and implementing mainstream disability rights programs and policies. This is not because Dubai is a typical case, but because it counters dominant thinking and provides a model in the areas of innovation, governance, inclusion, and urbanization. As such, ensuring that persons with disabilities/determination are entitled to all the rights and privileges, that they are respected and treated with dignity, and that their potential as empowered and productive members of society is now recognized by the UAE as a whole, as demonstrated by the launch of the UAE disability national strategy in 2017 followed by the city of Abu Dhabi launching its ambitious disability strategy in 2020.

Urbanization provides Dubai and Abu Dhabi the opportunity for social inclusion, equitable access to services and livelihoods, and engaging and mobilizing vulnerable populations at risk of exclusion. They are able to showcase efforts to combat social exclusion and marginalization and discuss how innovation and Universal Design projects in their cities are creating a new paradigm in inclusive urban development, collectively pledging that no one will be left behind. They denote that to operationalize the Leave No One Behind (LNOB) principle, local and regional governments should structure their policies around inclusive human rights instruments and development plans to include the CRPD, SDGs, New Urban Agenda (NUA), and the WHO Age-friendly Cities and Communities frameworks. Dubai's journey is a transformative model of inclusion. It has shaped the development of quality standards on inclusion and accessibility, underpinning the principles and mechanism of the Cities4All Global Compact on Inclusive and Accessible Cities framework for local and regional governments to begin developing and aligning their urban strategies toward inclusion. In practice, the six principles—non-discrimination, participation, accessibility, inclusive urban policies and programs, capacity building, and data for development—can lead to tangible shifts in social equity and resilience in cities and create universally inclusive and accessible environments that leave no one behind.

What Can We Learn from This Case Study?

The overall goal by passing the Dubai Disability Strategy in 2015 was to develop an inclusive, barrier-free, and rights-based framework that would allow the institutions to evolve and respond more effectively to the needs of persons with disabilities and older persons.

In light of these strategies and laws being passed first in Dubai, the Federal Government adopted them in policy, planning, and design, which made inclusion and accessibility part of the national federal strategy in

2020[19], shortly after the city of Abu Dhabi launched their Strategy for People of Determination. The implementation of these laws has just begun.

In particular, the coordinating mechanisms developed in Dubai were innovative; they created immediate and profound results. The Smart Dubai Agency, leading digital transformation, responded to the Dubai Disability Strategy by holding itself accountable to the highest rating in digital accessibility and adhering to the highest standards of accessibility in all government websites, apps, training programs, and other digital infrastructure.

In 2016, a coalition that included the Dubai Executive Council, the Roads & Transportation Authority, and the Community Development Authority started the Dubai Universal Accessibility Strategy and Action Plan (DUASAP) as a direct follow-up to the Dubai Disability Strategy. The goal was to ensure that the Emirate of Dubai becomes fully and universally accessible in preparation for Dubai Expo 2020. The process resulted in the Dubai Universal Design Code and a training program to transfer skills to architects and engineers working for the Dubai Municipality and all related government agencies. Further, this action plan affects how to audit the city infrastructure, identifying and addressing physical and social barriers to inclusion and accessibility.

In 2017, the Dubai Inclusive Education Policy Framework was launched by the Dubai Disability Strategy's Inclusive Education Task Force that aims to transform education systems to be inclusive. The policy framework for inclusive education, along with three additional support publications including guidelines for schools and parents, are directives from the Dubai Disabilities Strategy, which aims to make the city a fully cohesive and inclusive society, one where the rights and access to equitable opportunities for children with disabilities are assured and protected. The inclusive education framework is rights-based and in line with the UAE's local and federal legislation that fulfill obligations toward the United Nations Convention on the Rights of Persons with Disabilities (CRPD).

Callout Box—News Article

People with disabilities rate the top 10 cities that are easiest for them to travel around
Source: CNBC TRAVEL

---

[19] Note: More information about this exciting journey at Pineda, Victor (2020). Building the inclusive city: Governance, access, and the urban transformation of Dubai.

Consider This The Valuable 500, a business coalition, released its list of the top 10 most accessible cities in the world. The report cited a survey conducted among 3500 individuals with disabilities, who rated cities based on "transport links, proximity of accommodation to attractions, shops, and restaurants, and the availability of information about accessibility." The survey involved participants from five countries—the U.K., United States, Japan, China and Australia.

Martin Heng, a travel writer who wrote the report, noted: "Although physical accessibility is important, what's so significant is that across all territories people with disability choose travel providers based on being treated with respect and having an understanding of their needs." This highlights the importance of accessibility and inclusivity in the travel and tourism industry. Accessibility arrangements for individuals with disabilities are often an afterthought in the industry, and the survey shows that cities that consistently score well in accessibility rankings are those that provide accessible transport, information, and accommodations, and that treat individuals with disabilities with respect and have an awareness of their needs. Ensuring accessibility and inclusivity in the travel and tourism industry is not only important for the benefit of individuals with disabilities, but also for the industry as a whole, as it allows for a wider range of customers to access and enjoy its services.

References

Albarracín, D., Zanna, M. P., Johnson, B. T., & Kumakale, G. T. (2005). Attitudes: Introduction and scope. In D. Albarracín, B. T. Johnson, & M. P. Zanna (Eds.), *The Handbook of Attitudes* (pp. 3–20). Lawrence Erlbaum Associates Publishers.

Baumgartner, F. R., Jones, B. D., & Mortensen, P. B. (2018). Punctuated equilibrium theory: Explaining stability and change in public policymaking. *Theories of the Policy Process*, 55–101.

Fagence, M. (1977). *Citizen Participation in Planning*. Pergamon Press.

Farazmand, A. (2009). Building administrative capacity for the age of rapid globalization: A modest prescription for the twenty-first century. *Public Administration Review*, 69(6), 1007–1020.

Fleischer, D. Z., & Zames, F. (2011). *The Disability Rights Movement: From charity to confrontation*. Temple University Press. http://www.jstor.org/stable/j.ctt14bt7kv

Forester, J. (1993). *Critical theory, public policy, and planning practice*. State University of New York Press.

Habitat III. (n.d.-a). *Habitat III*. Retrieved May 19, 2023, from https://habitat3.org

Habitat III. (n.d.-b). *Issue Papers* Retrieved May 19, 2023, from https://habitat3.org/documents-and-archive/preparatory-documents/issue-papers/

Kratochwil, F. V. (1991). *Rules, norms, and decisions: On the conditions of practical and legal reasoning in international relations and domestic affairs*. Cambridge University Press.

Othering and Belonging Institute. (n.d.). *Home*. Retrieved May 19, 2023, from https://belonging.berkeley.edu/

Pineda, V. (2020). *Building the Inclusive City: Governance, access, and the urban transformation of Dubai*. Springer International Publishing. https://doi.org/10.1007/978-3-030-32988-4

Prince, M. J. (2008). Inclusive City Life: Persons with Disabilities and the Politics of Difference. *Society for Disability Studies, 2008*(1). https://dsq-sds.org/article/view/65/65

Schweik, S. M. (2010). *The Ugly Laws: Disability in public*. NYU Press.

Sen, A. (1999). *Commodities and capabilities*. Oxford University Press.

Wildavsky, A. B. (1986). *Budgeting: A comparative theory of the budgeting process*. Transaction Publishers.

Young, I. M. (2011). *Justice and the Politics of Difference*. Princeton University Press.

Open Access This chapter is licensed under the terms of the Creative Commons Attribution 4.0 International License (http://creativecommons.org/licenses/by/4.0/), which permits use, sharing, adaptation, distribution and reproduction in any medium or format, as long as you give appropriate credit to the original author(s) and the source, provide a link to the Creative Commons licence and indicate if changes were made.

The images or other third party material in this chapter are included in the chapter's Creative Commons licence, unless indicated otherwise in a credit line to the material. If material is not included in the chapter's Creative Commons licence and your intended use is not permitted by statutory regulation or exceeds the permitted use, you will need to obtain permission directly from the copyright holder.

CHAPTER 6

Emerging Trends in Cities of Tomorrow

Abstract The Fourth Industrial Revolution, which includes a range of technologies such as artificial intelligence, robotics, and biosensors, is already underway and is rapidly changing the way we live. While many of the technologies being implemented are unquestionably useful, the rate at which this transformation is occurring as well as the impacts many of these technologies are having on privacy and security is of great concern. The cities of the future will increasingly depend on these new technologies to provide services to all citizens. Emerging technologies offer opportunities for inclusive and accessible urban environments, but ongoing dialogue and collaboration between different stakeholders is necessary to ensure that the future of cities is equitable for all. For this transformation to be successful, governments need to monitor and assess the impact of emerging technologies on citizens, particularly those with disabilities and those most at risk of exclusion. Targeted universalism is an approach that aims to achieve universal goals through targeted interventions, taking into account the specific needs of each group while maintaining a universal policy goal. This approach considers both specialized and universal goals and measures progress that is customized for each community in order to advance equity and social development objectives.

Keywords Emerging technologies • Fourth Industrial Revolution • Targeted Universalism • Internet of Things • Urban policymakers • Transformation • Data security • Privacy

> We need to revisit the way we plan cities because it is becoming clear that adhering to best practices helps cities become more resilient places. More importantly, we must ensure inclusivity is at the heart of how we manage cities. We need to create a greater level of livability and embed inclusivity to ensure that everyone has equal access to housing and public spaces. We need to put people before profit. (Maimunah Mohd Sharif, Under-Secretary-General and Executive Director of UN-Habitat)

As I checked out of the Emirates Towers Hotel, I witnessed the construction of the museum of the future. I closed my eyes and imagined a day in the not-too-distant future when all our work on accessibility would come to life. Here's the story that I dreamed up that day: Fatima wakes up to the sound of her smart virtual assistant gently coaxing her out of bed. She smiles as she remembers the countless ways in which this technology has transformed her life.

As she gets dressed, she reaches for her white cane, which is always within easy reach. She knows that the smart city in which she lives is designed to be fully accessible to her, but she also knows that it never hurts to be prepared. As she steps outside, Fatima is immediately struck by the beauty of the city, it is described to her in rich visual descriptions by her Seeing AI enabled glasses. The buildings are sleek and modern, with clean lines and smooth surfaces. The streets are lined with lush trees and flowering plants, and the air is fresh and clean.

Fatima smiles as she feels the sun on her face. She knows that the city is designed to be responsive to her needs, and she can feel the warmth of the sun and the cool breeze on her skin. She gets a weather update and an autonomous vehicle pulls up and provides a visual description of the interior and her AI guides her in. She knows that this is just one of the countless ways in which the technology of the city enhances her life.

Her accessible vehicle is part of the public transportation system and as a disabled resident she gets a discount on her fare, Fatima is greeted by a friendly voice. "Good morning, Fatima," the voice says. "Where would you like to go today?"

Fatima smiles and replies, "I'm going to the library today. I want to check out some new books." They take off and the car continues playing her audio book where she left off.

The voice replies, "Very well. The library is just a short distance away. When we arrive, follow the path to the left, and you will be there in no time."

The radically inclusive cities of tomorrow will increasingly rely on technology to effectively understand, manage, and deliver the services that meet the needs of all their citizens. In this way, understanding the future of cities is really about understanding transformation, as cities integrate with an increasing number of tech devices, sensors, and systems. This emerging trend of an increasing reliance on technologies has strong impacts on inclusion. For this technology-driven transformation to be a success requires that governments monitor and assess all aspects of the impact of emerging technologies on citizens, especially persons with disabilities and those at most risk of exclusion. The main arguments to focus on here include:

1. The need for proactive and forward-thinking approaches to urban governance, planning, and design in the face of rapid technological change.
2. The importance of considering the potential impacts of emerging technologies on issues of inclusion and belonging including the potential of emerging technologies to unlock new opportunities. There is also the need to ensure that these technologies are used in a way that benefits all members of a community.
3. The role of urban policymakers, planners, and designers in shaping the future of cities and the need for them to be proactive and responsive in addressing issues of inclusion and belonging.
4. The need for ongoing dialogue and collaboration between different stakeholders (including policymakers, technologists, community members, and others) in order to ensure that the future of cities is inclusive and equitable for all.

CITIES OF TOMORROW

The two most important contributors to the idea of the "city of tomorrow" are Peter Hall and Le Cobusier. Peter Hall's seminal Cities of Tomorrow remains an unrivaled account of the history of planning in theory and practice, as well as of the social and economic problems and opportunities that gave rise to it. Now comprehensively revised, the fourth edition offers a perceptive, critical, and global history of urban planning and design throughout the twentieth century and beyond. But these visions could never have predicted the power and depth of social transformation that is occurring today. For their times, these thinkers were setting precedents. They laid out the vision that for better or worse led us to inherit an urban form that shaped cities in the twenty-first century.

Le Corbusier's The City Without Streets, and Urban Utopias of the 20th Century are two of the most important contributions to the examination of these ideas. A revised and updated edition of the classic text, Urban Utopias of the 20th Century, from one of the most notable figures in the field of urban planning and design offers an incisive, insightful, and unrivaled critical history of planning in theory and practice, as well as of the underlying socio-economic challenges and opportunities. Comprehensively revised to take account of abundant new research published over the last decade, it reviews the development of the modern planning movement over the entire span of the twentieth century and beyond. It draws on global examples throughout and weaves the author's own fascinating experiences into the text to illustrate this authoritative story of urban growth.[1]

Values, Priorities, and Targeted Universalism

We don't want universal policies anyways, we want universal goals. The goals should be universal, the policies should be targeted based on how we're situated within structures and stories… So this actually becomes not only operationally but also in terms of communication, a bridging strategy. In order to do it you have to explicate what structures are doing, how we're situated differently within structures, and what the universal is. And in doing so, you tell a story where everyone is in the story. (john powell, Director of the Othering & Belonging Institute at the University of California, Berkeley)

As cities grow and develop, they become the embodiment of society's values at a certain point in time. The values we hold are reflected in the places we build and the manner in which we design and provide services to people living in cities. By adopting a universal goal of radical inclusion in our quest to create resilient cities, we are taking a targeted universalist approach to identify which groups are being excluded. Targeted

---

[1] For those interested in diving deeper on related discussions that complement scholarship on Cities of Tomorrow, I suggest doing research on: Cities of Imagination, The Radical Roots of Urban Planning, The City of the Dreadful Night, The City of the Gardens, The City of the Commons, The City of Sweat Equity, The City of Theory, The City of the Permanent Underclass. These topics are outside the scope of the book but may illuminate new avenues for future research and ways that other urban scholars have addressed or failed to address persons with disabilities and/or other concepts presented in this book.

universalism provides the tools to understand specific interventions/lifestyles/choices that are situated within race, gender, class, and sexual orientation. It also incorporates factors such as geography, immigration status, and disability and identifies the axis from which equity can be leveraged, achieved, advanced, or improved.

Universalist approaches provide the same products, services, benefits, and protections to everyone irrespective of individual identity. Targeted approaches, in contrast, offer specific products/services/benefits/protections to certain groups/demographics who need them. For example, food stamps qualification depends on income level.

Targeted universalism combines these approaches by setting universal goals that can be achieved through targeted approaches. The approach targets the various needs of each group while reminding us that we are all part of the same social fabric.[2] It rejects a blanket universal, which may be indifferent to the reality that different groups are situated differently relative to the institutions and resources of society.[3]

Targeted universalism is a platform to operationalize programs that move all groups toward a universal policy goal as well as an effective way of communicating such programs in an inclusive manner. Using this approach, it is possible to support the needs of particular groups, even the politically powerful or those in the majority, while communicating to all stakeholders that they are all part of the same social fabric. This makes targeted universalist policies more resistant to critiques that a government program has been designed only to serve special interests, whoever they may be. Targeted universalistic interventions serve to overcome structural exclusion and marginalization of outgroups and instead promote tangible experiences of belonging that serve the needs of both outgroups and more powerful or favored groups.[4]

Targeted universalism means setting universal goals and using targeted processes to achieve those goals. It is a platform to operationalize programs that move all groups toward a universal policy goal as well as a way

---

[2] Powell, J. Ake, W. and Menendian, S., (2019). Targeted Universalism: Policy & Practice. *UC Berkeley: Othering & Belonging Institute.* Retrieved from https://escholarship.org/uc/item/9sm8b0q8

[3] *Othering and Belonging Institute, University of California, Berkeley,* Targeted Universalism: Animated Video + Curriculum, University of California, Berkeley. Accessed Nov 29 2022, available at: https://belonging.berkeley.edu/targeted-universalism-animated-video-curriculum

[4] See footnote 3.

of communicating and publicly marketing such programs in an inclusive, bridging manner.

The process by which it is carried out can be broken down into five steps:

1. Setting a universal goal
2. Measuring how the overall population fares relative to the goal
3. Measuring the performance of the population segments relative to the goal
4. Understanding how structures and other factors support or impede groups progress toward the universal goal
5. Implementing targeted strategies so that each group can achieve the universal goal based on their own needs and circumstances

A targeted universal strategy is one that is inclusive of the needs of both the dominant and marginal groups but pays particular attention to the situation of marginal groups. Targeted universalism rejects a blanket universal which is likely to be indifferent to the reality that different groups are situated differently relative to the institutions and resources of society. It also rejects the claim of formal equality that would treat all people the same as a way of denying difference. Any proposal would be evaluated by the outcome, not just the intent.

Among the core strengths of the targeted universalism framework is its potential for ingenuity and boldness in policy thinking, which opens up possibilities for experimentalist design in a more nuanced fashion that rejects "either-or" approaches. Targeted universalism requires us to consider both specialized approaches and universal goals. Can we measure progress that is both targeted and customized for each community, and yet advance broader based equity and social development objectives? How can we build access and governance by design? Below are a few considerations that allow urban practitioners to assess their programs, policies, and designs within a new radically inclusive approach. Systems that respond to and adapt to a user's needs will consider the following:

1. Body Fit: Accommodating a wide range of body sizes and abilities.
2. Comfort: Keeping demands within desirable limits of body function and perception.

3. Awareness: Ensuring that critical information for use is easily perceived.
4. Understanding: Making methods of operation and use intuitive, clear, and unambiguous.
5. Wellness: Contributing to health promotion, avoidance of disease, and protection from hazards.
6. Social Integration: Treating all groups with dignity and respect.
7. Personalization: Incorporating opportunities for choice and the expression of individual preferences.
8. Cultural appropriateness: Respecting and reinforcing cultural values, and the social and environmental contexts of any design project.

How Do We Make These Values Real?

In order for cities to become more inclusive and resilient, it is important to consider not only the values and principles that guide our efforts, but also the practical considerations of how to finance, manage, procure, operationalize, and construct new design and governance approaches. Innovations in financing, such as disability bonds and crowdfunding, can help to make these values a reality by providing access to lower cost financing and support for inclusive initiatives.

Innovations in financing will be vital. As identified by Ayman Seijiny, CEO, The Islamic Corporation for the Development of the Private Sector (ICD) of the Islamic Development Bank Group (IsDB):

> *One of the best opportunities that exist to better include people with disabilities as beneficiaries of project-based initiatives is to follow a similar process to that created with green bonds. These ultimately allow for lower cost financing and a similar approach can be used to issue disability bonds. It will be interesting to see how disability can be benefited by these types of funding models that could also for example include crowdfunding and other alternative financing options.*

The concept of "mobility as a service" can vastly improve accessibility for persons with disabilities or mobility limitations by providing on-demand transportation options and taking into consideration the entire mobility chain within a city. On-demand accessible taxi services, such as UberWAV and Lyft Access, which are wheelchair friendly and can be booked on short notice, are examples of this concept in action. By thinking holistically about the "mobility chain," cities can expand the scope of planning for accessible transport to include all the nodes that connect social and physical infrastructure, enabling smart mobility. For example, this could involve integrating accessible taxi services with public transportation, as well as providing accessible pedestrian and bicycle infrastructure, in order to create a seamless and inclusive transportation network.

New design approaches can be taken, such as those used in DeafSpace. DeafSpace is an example of how the lived experience of disability can shape the design and planning of cities to create more inclusive and accessible spaces. DeafSpace was designed with the cultural preferences and communication needs of deaf people in mind, using Universal Design principles as a framework. While DeafSpace is designed to be accessible and easy to navigate for deaf people, it also has features that make it more accessible for non-deaf people, such as ramps, wide pathways, and rounded turns. This approach to design and planning can serve as a case study for other communities with disabilities, such as those with autism or visual impairments, as it demonstrates the importance of considering the unique needs and experiences of these communities in the design process.

Similar approaches have been used in buildings such as the San Francisco Lighthouse for the Blind, designed by blind architect Chris Downey. By including the perspectives and input of underrepresented communities in the planning process, cities can create greater senses of belonging. Future planners and designers can use DeafSpace as a model for how to create sensory-friendly spaces that are accessible and welcoming to all. The impact of this work on the future of cities cannot be overstated as it advances radical inclusion and creates new design standards and innovations that prioritize the needs of all members of a community.

THE FOURTH INDUSTRIAL REVOLUTION

We are currently experiencing the Fourth Industrial Revolution. It is the digital revolution that is being built on top of the electronic and information technology revolutions that came before it. Klaus Schwab, Founder and Executive Chairman of the World Economic Forum, defines the Fourth Industrial Revolution as the rapid set of changes that are occurring to:

> *Create a world in which virtual and physical systems of manufacturing globally cooperate with each other in a flexible way. This enables the absolute customization of products and the creation of new operating models. The Fourth*

Industrial Revolution, however, is not only about smart and connected machines and systems. Its scope is much wider. Occurring simultaneously are waves of further breakthroughs in areas ranging from gene sequencing to nanotechnology, from renewables to quantum computing. It is the fusion of these technologies and their interaction across the physical, digital, and biological domains that make the Fourth Industrial Revolution fundamentally different from previous revolutions.[5]

The Fourth Industrial Revolution incorporates a whole range of technologies including biosensors, robotics, drones, blockchain, and artificial intelligence. It is a range of different forces that is shaping the ways that we will live and rewriting the equations of who is going to be empowered and who is going to be disempowered, who is going to be included and who is going to be excluded.

It is important to recognize that this current transformation has already been underway for many years. But the Fourth Industrial Revolution is the framework upon which we can understand how society's production capacity and the capability to produce value has changed, evolved, and merged with many other technologies that are currently under development and being piloted. Examples of these types of disruptive technologies include fully autonomous vehicles, 3D printing of complex parts, nanotechnology to produce miniaturized electronics, blockchain technologies,[6] and the use of quantum computing that will revolutionize drug research and development.

[5] Schwab, K. (2016). *The Fourth Industrial Revolution.* https://law.unimelb.edu.au/__data/assets/pdf_file/0005/3385454/Schwab-The_Fourth_Industrial_Revolution_Klaus_S.pdf

[6] The widespread uptake of blockchain technologies has the potential to revolutionize financial markets, data management and the data economy, privacy controls, and the digitization and tokenization of all forms of assets. This includes the transitions already underway with cities such as Dubai moving all property titles to the blockchain, but extends beyond record keeping to the tokenization of assets such as art, computing resources, and even the earning potential of athletes.

Blockchain also provides new opportunities for people who are underbanked or excluded from the financial system entirely as new options are emerging for these people to join the global economy and forge pathways out of poverty. This is beginning to be glimpsed through new forms of Web3 based income streams such as play-to-earn gaming opportunities where players, especially in developing nations, are earning a living through blockchain-powered gaming economies. This has major implications for people in developing countries as well as for persons with disabilities who may have previously been excluded from any genuine income generating possibilities.

Emerging technologies have the potential to advance urban access and inclusion, and promote radical inclusion, which is the idea that everyone, regardless of background or ability, should have access to the same opportunities and experiences. Here are some innovative approaches that are leveraging emerging technologies:

Augmented Reality (AR) and Virtual Reality (VR): AR and VR technologies can be used to create immersive and inclusive experiences that help people with disabilities, including those with autism, navigate and access public spaces. For example, AR and VR can be used to create virtual guides that provide step-by-step instructions on how to navigate public transportation or locate accessible entrances to buildings.

Internet of Things (IoT): IoT technologies can be used to create more inclusive and accessible environments, such as smart homes and buildings that can be customized to meet the needs of people with disabilities. For example, sensors and smart devices can be used to automate tasks, such as turning on lights or adjusting the thermostat, to make homes more accessible and comfortable for people with disabilities.

Machine Learning (ML) and Artificial Intelligence (AI): ML and AI can be used to create more personalized and inclusive experiences for people with disabilities. For example, ML and AI can be used to develop speech recognition technologies that can adapt to different accents and dialects, making it easier for people with speech impairments to communicate.

Open data for mobile apps: Open data on accessibility can power a new generation of mobile apps. For example, Accessibility.Cloud[7] managed by Sozialhelden in Berlin has crowdsourced tens of millions of GIS data points on accessibility. Initiatives such as this can be used to create more accessible and inclusive environments, such as apps that provide real-time information on accessible routes or accessible parking spots. Mobile apps can also be used to promote inclusive experiences, such as apps that provide information on accessible events and activities in the community.

Social media: Social media can be used to promote radical inclusion by providing a platform for people with disabilities to connect with each

---

[7] Accessibility Cloud is an initiative that allowed for massive integration and the development of standards around geo-tagged accessibility data. It was supported by Google and has been integrated into Google maps to support accessible routing in select cities.

other and share their experiences. Social media can also be used to raise awareness and promote advocacy for disability rights and inclusion.

Blockchain: Blockchain technology can be used to create more inclusive and secure systems for managing identity and financial transactions. For example, blockchain-based systems can be used to create digital identities that are secure and easily verifiable, making it easier for people with disabilities to access services and participate in the economy. This can be especially important for people with disabilities who may face challenges in accessing traditional financial systems, such as those who are unbanked or underbanked.

Blockchain technology can create more transparent and accountable systems for managing individual identities and accessing public resources, such as public transportation or affordable housing. By using blockchain-based systems to track the use of public resources, it becomes easier to identify areas where resources are not being used effectively and make changes to ensure that everyone has equal access to these resources.

By effectively governing the development and distribution of these emerging technologies, radical inclusion is no longer an idea, it can be a fact and a mechanism to unlock human potential and broaden the base of engagement through more equitable access to the public realm.

Technology-Driven Transformation

> *The rapid growth of technology is currently being accelerated right now faster than at any point in time due to the current COVID-19 crisis. Because of this crisis, all of us are working from home and able to continue with our day to day lives because of technology. The internet, video conferencing, and connected devices are allowing city governments, companies and businesses to continue to operate today.* (Jeff Merritt, Head for IOT, Robotics, Smart Cities Center for the Fourth Industrial Revolution, World Economic Forum)

The current technology-led transformation we are experiencing includes the Internet of Things (IoT), which is an entire system of interrelated computing devices. These are both mechanical and digital machines that transfer data over a network without requiring human-to-human or human-to-computer interaction. As a result, there are now already more connected devices in the world today than there are humans.

The sheer number of IoT devices already deployed creates some cause for concern. There is a clear need to guarantee data security and privacy. While these new technologies are an integral part of lives, there is also a need to ensure technologies such as AI and Big Data also protect our human rights.

Innovations in technology are unleashing new approaches to inclusive urban development. Additional focus needs to be put toward data management and ownership (including data collection, data cleaning, data structuring, and the deployment of accessibility data standards) in the provision of city services. This impacts data sharing, data storage, data analysis based on accessibility related problem sets, diverse personas, and vital scenario planning (like inclusive emergency preparedness) that the city is trying to resolve.

Accessibility in digital transformation efforts can also help improve transparency, accountability, and reach of public services to all. Furthermore, digital accessibility can help unlock new user insights and offer data needed to improve policy deliberations and measure in a disaggregated manner the realization of existing global commitments. It can also provide context-specific methods of assessing negative social attitudes, as well as mobilizing civil society to address complex factors and persistent challenges.

We need to create a set of norms that should be driving technologies such as AI, robotics, and Big Data to ensure these technologies are used virtuously in an inclusive and transparent way. We should be able to monitor the social impact of these technologies as we deploy them. This needs to occur in virtual sandboxes or policy sandboxes as we experiment with their uses, benefits, and potential drawbacks.

We are moving faster in the transformation than we are in regulating that transformation. So we must ensure that the prevention of social harm is prioritized. We must also ensure that the rollout or uptake of these technologies is done in a way that prevents discrimination or the reinforcement of inequalities on marginalized groups or those most at risk of exclusion.

Agile Cities and Buildings

In the Fourth Industrial Revolution, cities are shifting their focus from building up infrastructure and systems to making those systems more accessible and adaptable to changing citizen needs and new technologies. Agile cities are those that embrace transformation and use data-driven approaches to deliver services and support their citizens in a rapidly changing world. Agile cities are flexible and responsive, with a willingness to rezone land for more responsive and temporary uses, a mix of buildings with multiple functions, smart and data-driven policing and prevention strategies, accessible and interoperable transport systems that are optimized by real-time information, energy networks that maximize the use of renewables and protect vulnerable populations (like people who need power for medical reasons), and education systems that adapt to the specific needs of students (student centric) as well as the changing needs of the economy.

Physical Elements:

- Incorporating accessible design features such as ramps and elevators in public buildings and transportation systems to better serve individuals with disabilities.
- Developing green infrastructure, such as rooftop gardens and green walls, to improve air quality and reduce the urban heat island effect.
- Implementing smart traffic management systems, such as traffic sensors and variable speed limits, to reduce congestion and improve mobility in urban areas.

Digital Elements:

- Using smart city technologies, such as sensors and data analytics, to improve the efficiency and sustainability of urban services, such as waste management and energy distribution.
- Leveraging the Internet of Things (IoT) to create connected, responsive public spaces that can adapt to changing citizen needs, such as providing real-time information on transportation options and traffic conditions.
- Integrating artificial intelligence (AI) and machine learning algorithms into urban planning and decision-making processes to better understand and anticipate citizen needs and preferences.

Environmental Factors:

- Implementing low-carbon transportation systems, such as electric buses and bike-sharing programs, to reduce greenhouse gas emissions and improve air quality.

- Developing green buildings, such as those that use renewable energy sources and incorporate sustainable design features, to reduce the environmental impact of urban development.
- Investing in nature-based solutions, such as urban forests and green roofs, to mitigate the effects of climate change and improve the health and wellbeing of urban residents.

Inclusive Innovation:

- Engaging with diverse communities and stakeholders to co-design and co-create urban solutions that meet the needs and preferences of a wide range of individuals.
- Investing in technology and digital literacy programs to ensure that all citizens have equal access to the benefits of new technologies.
- Developing policies and programs that support the participation of underrepresented groups, such as women, low-income individuals, and people with disabilities, in urban decision-making processes and innovation initiatives.[8]

These concepts must also extend to the buildings within agile cities. Agile buildings are carbon-neutral, energy positive, technically sophisticated, and support a diverse mix of uses and activities through flexible space usage and shared working arrangements. They embrace the concept of "total building performance," which evaluates building performance based on six core categories of design—spatial, acoustic, visual, thermal, indoor air quality (IAQ), and building integrity.

Agile buildings create market incentives for the transformation of old and underperforming building stock according to six key performance indicators: carbon reduction, energy independence, occupant health, integration with urban infrastructure, real-time performance monitoring, and system interoperability. Agile buildings leverage Big Data and real-time monitoring, making extensive use of the latest in sensor technology and leaning heavily on principles such as interoperability and passive design. Through transit-oriented design, they encourage walkability and provide easy access to mass transportation.

---

[8] Preparing for the Fourth Industrial Revolution. In *World Economic Forum's (WEF) Global Future Council on Cities and Urbanization.–2018.* https://www3.weforum.org/docs/WP_Global_Future_Council_Cities_Urbanization_report_2018.pdf

Engineering New Approaches Through Partnerships

Due to the extensive fragmentation inherent in the architectural and engineering disciplines of the construction industry, partnering can be of great value to owners, agencies, government, private developers, and all other stakeholders. Unlike project delivery methods with a greater focus on team collaboration via relational contracts, project partnering can be utilized as a means of promoting collaboration and integration under any type of project delivery method. It therefore provides great opportunities to improve team integration across all types of projects, including public ones that require low-bid procurement and are delivered using the design-bid-build arrangement.[9] Partnering also offers a highly effective means of integrating the knowledge and expertise of disabled persons organizations in implementing accessibility standards and measures into major developments.

The motto, "Nothing about us without us" has evolved into the simple phrase, "Nothing without us." Persons with disabilities should be engaged along the supply chain, and organizations representing the needs of persons with disabilities need to enter partnerships with developers within the construction industry. The greatest shortcoming can be found in relation to architects, who often fail to consider the lifetime approach to the spaces they build and in some cases are hostile to access features that they feel may cloud their vision for spaces that may meet a particular esthetic but are poorly suited to the needs of a large part of the population who will be actually using that space. As Raymond Lichez stated in the opening of his vital work, Design for Independent Living, architecture should be the "thoughtful structuring of places to inhabit. It should be enabling. The architect should make it possible for people to have encounters with the environment that make them able to do more, to know more, to experience the world in ways that augment, rather than diminish, their sense of dignity and competence and joy, and that awaken their interest in one another."[10]

Design firms that center on Universal Design have created some of the most beautiful and forward looking buildings. However, they struggle to

---

[9] Mollaoglu, S., Sparkling, A. and Thomas, S., (2015). An inquiry to move an underutilized best practice forward: Barriers to partnering in the architecture, engineering, and construction industry. *Project management journal*, 46(1), pp. 69–83.

[10] Lifchez, R. and Winslow, B., (1981). Design for independent living: The environment and physically disabled people. *Univ of California Press*.

find the right partners in engineering and construction industries who have practical experience interpreting and operationalizing the vision for these "inclusive and accessible spaces." Partnerships should be based on a common set of values and disabled persons organizations should be supported and paid as expert consultants. Over 40 years ago, Professor Raymond Lichez brought new approaches to the architecture studio course he taught at the University of California Berkeley. He championed the creation of diverse and integrated teams that placed disabled residents as expert consultants. These disabled residents were treated as expert consultants and paid for their time. They supported students through designing a variety of spaces and projects. Many of these students have since gone on to be successful architects that have these sensibilities in mind. Firms and cities should be doing the same.

Training and sensitization are also vital across teams, and having the right technical advisors can save a project. However, too often we think about a climate advisor, or a gender advisor, while accessibility gets overlooked. These advisors can provide support, but the long-term capabilities should also be built internally through continuous learning, education, and training. This was vital in Abu Dhabi where there was a need to understand and disseminate knowledge across 26 agencies across the emirate. The knowledge was strongly tied to adopting KPIs and indicators in alignment with global frameworks in order to ensure the development and implementation of evidence based policies and programs. In particular, the specific requirements of the UNCRPD and the inclusion targets of the Sustainable Development Goals were customized across the governmental agencies to fulfill global mandates along with policy/program goals at the emirate level. Ultimately, the capacity building program over a two-year span allowed city officials, policymakers, and service providers to develop strong internal expertise, consolidating a more inclusive organizational ethos along with inclusive development policy and programs approaches and tools. This creates an ecosystem equipped to deliver on inclusion mandates and builds a new sense of pride for the future: A future for all.

The City Architect of Yerevan, Armenia once told me the following story. "I used to think these disabled activists were so annoying, always complaining, until I actually saw the challenges myself. Instead of looking at their inputs as complaints, I saw their knowledge as an asset and created a process by which the disability rights groups would partner with the city on infrastructure upgrading. They would be hired to identify, prioritize, and then supervise the execution of infrastructure improvements in the center of the city. They would also hold the purse strings and would need to sign off on completed projects for the contractor to be paid. That would ensure the public resources were used correctly, and the final results met the needs of the users. We now have a productive relationship with these groups and value their input and understanding of the communities they serve."

Data-Driven Urban Planning and Governance

Cities are complex systems, with many interconnected components that influence one another. Urban planners, policymakers, designers, and construction managers have long used data and analytics to understand and address the challenges facing cities. In recent years, advances in data science and machine learning capabilities have enabled the development of new algorithms and more powerful analytics systems that can help us better understand and govern urban environments. However, the use of data and algorithms in urban governance also raises important questions about potential bias and discrimination. Here, we will explore the potential of data and algorithms to improve urban planning, design, and construction, and identify the challenges and ethical considerations associated with their use.

The role of data and algorithms in urban governance, urban planning, and urban design and construction is expanding. This is due to the fact that the volumes of city-derived data are increasing as are the capabilities of data analytics and artificial intelligence to process and derive insights from this data. These tools are being used to collect, analyze, and interpret enormous amounts of data in order to make better informed decisions about the design, development, and management of cities.

Data and Algorithms in Urban Planning and Governance
One of the earliest examples of utilizing data analytics and AI to significant benefit was in the realm of transportation planning. By collecting data on traffic patterns, travel times, and congestion levels, urban planners began using data analytics and AI algorithms to develop more efficient transportation systems. This included everything from optimizing traffic light timing to predicting demand for public transit services. This use case will continue to expand significantly as the development and rollout of self-driving vehicles continues. This also extends to the optimization of public transportation routes and schedules. By analyzing data on the movement

of people throughout the city, urban planners can design transportation systems that are more efficient and accessible, benefiting both citizens and the environment.

Another area where data analytics and AI are being utilized is in the planning and management of public services. By analyzing data on demographics, population density, and other factors, city officials can use AI algorithms to identify areas where services are needed and allocate resources more effectively. This can for example be applied to predicting demand for healthcare services and schools within a city's regions. Some of the key benefits of using data and algorithms for urban governance purposes include improved decision-making, more efficient resource allocation, and enhanced resilience to environmental and social challenges. It can also be used to identify areas of a city with high concentrations of disadvantaged communities. This information can help allocate targeted resources and services, such as affordable housing and healthcare, to those areas in order to improve the wellbeing of the citizens living there.

Data and Algorithms in Urban Design and Construction
There is a need to further explore the use of data and algorithms in urban design and construction including architecture, landscape architecture, public space design, and construction management. Some areas where these techniques are already being beneficially used are in Building Information Modeling (BIM) and in the construction process itself. BIM allows for the production of a digital representation of the physical and functional characteristics of a building, which allows architects, engineers, and construction professionals to analyze and simulate a building's performance before it is built. By using data analytics and algorithms, BIM can help identify potential problems and design more efficient and sustainable buildings. Similarly, by using data analytics and algorithms in the construction process itself, construction companies can identify inefficiencies and optimize their processes. By collecting data on materials, labor, and other factors, construction companies can help reduce waste, improve safety, and speed up construction times, making the entire process more efficient and cost-effective.

Future researchers should explore how data and algorithms can be used at greater scale to inform and evaluate design and construction decisions and discuss the potential benefits and drawbacks of these approaches. Unless we address the challenges of incorporating data and algorithms into the design and construction process we will continue to further inequality and exclusion.

Data-driven urban planning and governance can also be used to create more inclusive and accessible public spaces. For instance, by analyzing data on the demographics and needs of a city's population, urban planners can design parks and other public spaces that are accessible to people with disabilities and meet the diverse needs of the community.

Overall, data-driven urban planning and governance can advance belonging, inclusion, and overall wellbeing for citizens by enabling cities to target resources and services to those who need them most, optimize public systems and infrastructure, and create more inclusive and accessible public spaces.

Drawbacks and Ethical Concerns

One of the greatest shortcomings of a reliance on data driven urban planning and governance is the possibility of bias and discrimination in the data and algorithms used. This can lead to further bias and discrimination against marginalized groups where the algorithms used were trained on biased data. If the data used to train an algorithm is biased, the algorithm will learn to reproduce that bias and make decisions that are unfair or discriminatory toward certain groups. For example, if an algorithm used for housing allocation is trained on data that reflects existing patterns of segregation and discrimination, it may perpetuate those biases and exclude people with disabilities from certain neighborhoods or housing opportunities.

Another way that data-driven urban planning and governance can lead to bias and discrimination is through the lack of representation and inclusion in the decision-making process. Data-driven approaches to urban planning and governance often rely on data collected from a limited and potentially unrepresentative sample of the population. If certain groups, including people with disabilities, are not included in the data collection and decision-making process, their needs and concerns may not be taken into account. This can result in urban policies and practices that are not inclusive or accessible, and that exacerbate existing inequalities and discrimination. In order to address these types of concerns, strategies need to be put in place that can mitigate bias and discrimination in data-driven urban governance, such as through dedicated data auditing and bias detection exercises that lead to the use of diverse and inclusive data sets.

Overall, the use of data analytics and AI-based algorithms is enabling urban planners and city officials to make more informed, data-driven decisions about the development and management of cities. Provided there is good oversight of the data collection and interpretation processes used, this can lead to more efficient, sustainable, and livable urban environments for all residents. But it is vital that the risks and drawbacks of using these approaches and technologies are recognized and measures put in place that actively ensure that the data sourced is accurate and inclusive of all of a city's residents.

Callout Box—News Article

Digital twin cities: The new frontier on our connected streets
Source: The Mandarin

Consider This Combined with the smart city movement, new macroeconomic conditions have prompted governments all over the world to invest in the planning and development of modern cities that reimagine the way we live and work. But rebuilding busy, often congested cities, while keeping them functioning is a challenging and sometimes expensive proposition. While urban planners and governments have been collecting big-picture data for some time, new technologies are encouraging the capture of ever more granular data. This enables initiatives such as "digital twins" that can help in planning efforts by comparing cities with national or global counterparts.

The use of data-driven intelligence and digital twins in urban planning is changing the way cities are built and rebuilt, allowing for more efficient and sustainable solutions to be developed. Digital twins allow urban planners to simulate proposed designs and test their impact on a city's environment, while data-driven intelligence allows for the capture of granular data on factors such as the movement of traffic or people or the distribution of canopy cover or public facilities to inform planning decisions. These approaches are being used in cities around the world to address issues such as traffic congestion, unaffordable housing, vandalism and youth crime, accessibility, and environmental degradation. The global smart cities market is expected to grow significantly in the coming years, with a focus on using technology and data to create cleaner, better connected, more sustainable, and more inclusive urban environments.

References

Global Future Council on Cities and Urbanization. (2018, September). *Agile Cities: Preparing for the Fourth Industrial Revolution*. World Economic Forum. Retrieved May 20, 2023, from https://www.weforum.org/whitepapers/agile-cities-preparing-for-the-fourth-industrial-revolution/

Lifchez, R., & Winslow, B. (1981). *Design for independent living: The environment and physically disabled people*. University of California Press.

Mollaoglu, S., Sparkling, A., & Thomas, S. (2015). An inquiry to move an underutilized best practice forward: Barriers to partnering in the architecture, engineering, and construction industry. *Project Management Journal, 46*(1), 69–83.

Othering & Belonging Institute. (2017, February 8). *Targeted Universalism: Animated Video*. Retrieved May 20, 2023, from https://belonging.berkeley.edu/targeted-universalism-animated-video

Othering and Belonging Institute. (2019). *New primer: Targeted universalism opens pathways for policy innovation*. https://belonging.berkeley.edu/tu-press-release

Pineda, V. (2020). *Building the Inclusive City: Governance, Access, and the Urban Transformation of Dubai*. Palgrave Springer. https://link.springer.com/book/10.1007/978-3-030-32988-4

powell, john a., Ake, W., & Menendian, S. (2019). *Targeted Universalism: Policy & Practice*. https://escholarship.org/uc/item/9sm8b0q8

powell, john a. (2020). Post-Racialism or Targeted Universalism. *Denver Law Review, 86*(3).

Schwab, K. (2016). *The Fourth Industrial Revolution*. World Economic Forum. https://law.unimelb.edu.au/__data/assets/pdf_file/0005/3385454/Schwab-The_Fourth_Industrial_Revolution_Klaus_S.pdf

Open Access This chapter is licensed under the terms of the Creative Commons Attribution 4.0 International License (http://creativecommons.org/licenses/by/4.0/), which permits use, sharing, adaptation, distribution and reproduction in any medium or format, as long as you give appropriate credit to the original author(s) and the source, provide a link to the Creative Commons licence and indicate if changes were made.

The images or other third party material in this chapter are included in the chapter's Creative Commons licence, unless indicated otherwise in a credit line to the material. If material is not included in the chapter's Creative Commons licence and your intended use is not permitted by statutory regulation or exceeds the permitted use, you will need to obtain permission directly from the copyright holder.

CHAPTER 7

The Era of the New Normal

Abstract Leading smart cities are transforming their urban planning processes by building inclusion and access into their city-wide master plans. This is resulting in cities that are more accessible, inclusive, and resilient. A key factor in this journey is the adoption of key principles of resilience in their decision-making and planning processes: reflection, resourcefulness, inclusivity, integration, robustness, redundancy, and flexibility. Inclusivity is crucial in building resilience as cities need to prioritize broad consultation and create a sense of shared ownership in decision-making to ensure the needs and perspectives of all members of the community are taken into account. This is complemented by the use of human-rights based regulatory frameworks, agile regulatory structures, collaboration with civil society organizations, and continuous learning, training, and upskilling. Cities should reflect on past experiences to inform future decisions. Universal Design principles can also enhance the effectiveness of radical inclusion efforts. The practice of Universal Design has expanded greatly to include policy, social participation, and health and wellness. The ultimate success of these initiatives is also largely dependent on the ability of cities to effectively adopt and integrate technologies in a way that supports the needs of all citizens.

Keywords Resilience • Inclusivity • Integration • Flexibility • Smart cities • Emerging technologies • Agile regulatory structures • Universal Design

> *I think it is undeniable that digital transformation is creating right now, winners and losers. We must be capable of reverting this tendency in order to make the digital transition in the service of human rights. We must seek to reduce social inequalities and bet on the creation of a model of the digital city that is accessible and will leave no one behind. In other words, we cannot allow that the process of digitization merely finishes consolidating a new face of inequality. And that is in our hands.* (Laia Bonet, Deputy Mayor of Barcelona)

One way that cities can be accessible, inclusive, and resilient in the "new normal" is by adopting the key principles of resilience in their decision-making and planning processes. By reflecting on past experiences, cities can learn from their successes and challenges in order to inform future decisions. This can help them to be resourceful and recognize alternative ways to utilize their resources. These principles existed before the pandemic but emerged as a source of greater urban resilience.

Inclusivity is essential in building resilience, as cities should prioritize broad consultation and create a sense of shared ownership in decision-making. This ensures that the needs and perspectives of all members of the community are taken into account and can help to build trust and collaboration. Furthermore, cities should strive for integration by bringing together a range of distinct systems and institutions. This can help ensure that different parts of the city are working together toward a common goal and can enhance the overall resilience of the city.

In addition to these principles, cities should also focus on building robust and redundant systems and maintaining flexibility in order to adapt to changing circumstances. By adopting these strategies, cities can become more accessible, inclusive, and resilient in the "new normal."[1]

The following seven principles can help guide us toward a more radically inclusive and by extension, a more resilient urban future. The seven principles are further elaborated in the sections below.[2]

1. **Reflection**—using past experiences to inform future decisions
2. **Resourcefulness**—recognizing alternative ways to utilize resources

---

[1] For more content in this area, see Cheshmehzangi, A. (2020). *The City in Need*. Springer Singapore. New scholarship being led by my colleague Dr. Serida Catalano will explore the new normal through the lens of neurodiversity in environmental design, watch for this important research and upcoming publications.

[2] Pineda, V., (2020). Resilience and Recovery Strategies for People with Disabilities in Response to a Pandemic, *LinkedIn post*. https://www.linkedin.com/pulse/resilience-recovery-strategies-people-disabilities-response-pineda/

3. **Inclusivity**—prioritizing broad consultation to create a sense of shared ownership in decision-making
4. **Integration**—bringing together a range of distinct systems and institutions
5. **Robustness**—well-conceived, constructed, and managed systems
6. **Redundancy**—spare capacity purposefully created to accommodate disruption
7. **Flexibility**—willingness and ability to adopt alternative strategies in response to changing circumstances

In order to increase reflection, cities and city leaders can use a variety of tools and techniques to analyze their past experiences and learn from them. For example, they could conduct regular evaluations and assessments of their programs and initiatives and use this information to inform future decision-making. Cities could also establish mechanisms for feedback and input from citizens and stakeholders, such as surveys, focus groups, and community meetings.

To increase resourcefulness, cities can adopt a creative and innovative approach to using their resources. This could involve identifying new sources of funding and support, such as partnerships with businesses and organizations, or exploring alternative financing mechanisms such as crowdfunding or social impact bonds. Cities could also look for opportunities to share resources and services with other municipalities, in order to reduce costs and increase efficiency.

Inclusivity can be enhanced by prioritizing broad consultation and involving a diverse range of stakeholders in decision-making. Cities could establish advisory committees or task forces that bring together representatives from different sectors and communities and provide a platform for them to share their perspectives and ideas. Cities could also use digital tools and platforms, such as online forums and social media, to engage with a wider range of citizens and stakeholders. This naturally extends to improving governance as well as a sense of belonging for those who have participated in the consultation process.

To increase integration, cities can work to foster collaboration and coordination among different systems and institutions. This could involve establishing interagency agreements and partnerships and creating mechanisms for sharing information and resources. Cities could also develop and implement city-wide plans and strategies that take into account the needs and priorities of all sectors and stakeholders.

To increase robustness, cities can focus on designing and implementing well-conceived, constructed, and managed systems. This could involve investing in infrastructure and services that are resilient to natural disasters and other disruptions and adopting best practices in project management and risk assessment. Cities could also establish clear policies and procedures for maintaining and upgrading their systems over time.

To increase redundancy, cities can create spare capacity in their systems and infrastructure in order to accommodate disruption. This could involve designing buildings and infrastructure with multiple redundant systems or establishing backup power sources and other contingency plans. Cities could also invest in technologies and systems that are scalable and flexible, in order to adapt to changing circumstances and demands. This provides better long-term access, no matter what situations arise as systems become more resilient.

Finally, to increase flexibility, cities can foster a culture of adaptability and innovation and be willing to try new approaches and strategies in response to changing circumstances. Cities could establish mechanisms for experimentation on inclusive innovation, such as incubators, accelerators, and innovation labs that all value and advance social inclusion and social resilience. Such approaches are radical in the sense that they provide support and resources for entrepreneurs and innovators dedicated to building new social systems, new structures to bring people into a productive and more equitable social standing viz a viz their more established or privileged peers. Cities could also create policies and processes that enable them to quickly adapt to new challenges and opportunities as they relate to social exclusion, discrimination, and other human rights violations.

Enhancing radical inclusion enhances urban resilience. Both of these also present wider opportunities for cities to better utilize their resources and capabilities beyond the scope of the pandemic.

Emerging Trends Accelerating the Speed of Urban Transformation

The effects of the COVID-19 pandemic created many sudden changes to the ways we carried out our lives. Some of the most important of these included: rapid adoption of remote working; greater data privacy considerations posed by COVID-19 tracking apps; using hotels to house people experiencing homeless; increased strain on digital infrastructure;

acceleration in the adoption of automation; transition to virtual service delivery; the shift to participatory, virtual cultural experiences; the flourishing of open innovation; isolation intensifying mental health challenges; and new financing needs and models.

Each of these shifts provided clear risks as well as opportunities for cities and societies. These changes can also have exaggerated impacts on at-risk people including people with disabilities and older people as they are often the last people considered when sudden trends emerge and society has little time to enact proper planning.

However, these new trends also provide the opportunity to use these changes as a way to alter the course of the greater transformations underway. For example, by making these changes to work practices, data privacy measures, accommodation, and service delivery properly consider those most at risk so that the longer-term adaptations that society is forced to make to deal with major events like the COVID-19 pandemic ultimately result in greater equity and accessibility for all.

SMART CITIES ARE ACCESSIBLE CITIES

> *When Hurricane Sandy hit New York City in 2012, it hit hard. The city wasn't as prepared as it is today. There were issues with shelters, issues with getting communications out, and issues around paying attention to persons with disabilities to the level that was needed. That has now changed.* (Victor Calise, Commissioner of NYC Mayor's Office of Persons with Disabilities)

The types of programs and infrastructure investments best suited for deployment in each city vary depending on the local circumstances of that city. This includes a range of factors such as location, population size, demographics, etc. But there is much that can be learned from the approaches and projects that have already been successfully deployed in smart cities around the world.

New York, United States
New York City was considered the epicenter of the COVID-19 pandemic in the United States. Its high initial case numbers and fatalities meant it was required to take the lead in the pandemic response and many of the lessons learned were applied to other cities in the United States and around the world as cases continue to spread.

When comparing New York City's level of preparedness for the COVID-19 pandemic with that at the time of Hurricane Sandy in 2012, the city was far better equipped to assist persons with disabilities. Some of the measures it put in place in response to the pandemic included:

1. **Accessible platforms and communications**—every video that the City of New York puts out has captioning and sign language is available at all mayoral press conferences.
2. **Weekly stakeholders meetings**—to get back to people with direct responses to questions.
3. **Accessible transportation**—access to a para transport shared ride system, an e-health system to order taxis on demand, and accessible buses where persons with disabilities and older persons have a dedicated access point at the front of buses.
4. **Permitting**—extended permits to allow persons with disabilities to park all over the city and extended timeframe allowances.
5. **Essential workers**—health care workers and personal care assistants were formally declared as essential workers.
6. **Education**—the city has over 250,000 individual education plans for children with special learning needs. This was extended to include e-learning platforms so that children have access to accessible laptops and the internet.
7. **Food distribution**—platforms to access food for those in need as well as food distribution via taxis to those with limited mobility.
8. **Senior hours**—dedicated hours when grocery stores were open exclusively for older persons.

The New York City Mayor's Office of Persons with Disabilities (NYC MOPD) has created an accessible virtual meeting guide to educate public and private partners to be equitable when hosting public meetings. The NYC transportation network includes a variety of accessible services including access to a para transport shared ride system, an e-health system to order taxis on demand, and accessible buses where persons with disabilities and older persons have a dedicated access point at the front of buses. The city's Office of Emergency Management Unit also has a Disability Access Functional Needs (DAFN) section to work directly with NYC MOPD and their community stakeholders to ensure the City's emergency response plans include persons with disabilities.

Barcelona, Spain
Nearly 40 years ago, Barcelona established the National Municipal Institute of People with Disabilities (IMPD). The institute is a dedicated organization leading the improvement of mobility and accessibility in Barcelona. It has helped transform an industrial, working class city into a modern, accessible city for all.

The first major accessibility policy developed for the city was the installation of ramps on all the sidewalks and zebra crossings. Today, nearly 100 percent of all the zebra crossings in the city are accessible. The next major development was a dedication to accessible public transport to ensure persons with disabilities in the city could use the buses, trolley cars, and subway. This was a very significant investment as it meant replacing the entire fleet of buses used in the city. It was then followed by the installation of elevators within the subway system to allow for direct access from the street level to the station lobbies, and from the lobbies to the platform. This is still a surprisingly lacking feature of most major cities around the world. But today, around 80 percent of the metro stations in Barcelona are fully accessible. The remaining stations are the oldest stations that have more complex infrastructure because of their antiquity.

The city now also has a dedicated team of 40 people with reduced mobility that continuously travel the city. Each team is tasked with the ongoing evaluation of the accessibility of the city. All areas are checked and tested by these teams to develop a priority list of public spaces or locations that require the most urgent work to address accessibility issues.

Singapore
Singapore has long had a strong reputation for creating well planned city infrastructure and services. It has a coordinated transport system that includes trains, buses, taxis, bicycles, and Grabs (private service cars). Its workforce development services provide opportunities to develop the skills of workers of all ages, genders, and abilities to improve their career prospects. These services include strategic services for businesses whether employers are expanding or reducing their workforces. Singapore has also focused on building a strong foundation for digital inclusion through initiatives such as the National Digital Literacy Programme, which provides training and support to help citizens develop the skills and knowledge they need to fully participate in the digital economy.

Singapore's response to the COVID-19 pandemic was also lauded as one of the most effective globally, which is partly due to its prior dedication to Universal Design and the deployment of accessible and equitable city services. When the pandemic hit, it initiated a comprehensive plan to ensure that essential community services remained available, especially for the people who most needed them. This included ensuring all public and private acute hospitals and community hospitals remained open for the delivery of essential services/procedures. Residential and home-based community care services such as nursing homes, psychiatric rehabilitation homes, psychiatric sheltered homes, inpatient palliative care, home medical, home nursing, home palliative care, interim caregiver service, homes for the disabled, and meals delivery services continued to function. Educational services across both mainstream and special schools provided by the Ministry of Education (MOE) also ensured Full Home-Based Learning (HBL) programs were in place during periods of full or partial lockdowns.

Dubai, UAE
Dubai has placed great emphasis on creating a dynamic, vibrant, and inclusive smart city through the use of emerging technologies such as artificial intelligence, blockchain, and autonomous vehicles. The aims of Dubai's smart city initiative are to improve the quality of life for all citizens, including those with disabilities. To this end, Dubai has developed the Dubai Disability Strategy, which aims to create an inclusive and accessible environment for all. The strategy includes a range of initiatives, such as the development of accessible infrastructure and the use of assistive technologies, to enable people with disabilities to fully participate in all aspects of life in the city.

One example of how emerging technologies can support the goals of the Dubai Disability Strategy is the use of AI and blockchain to improve the efficiency and accessibility of government services. For example, the use of blockchain technology to facilitate the secure and permanent record keeping of visa applications, bill payments, license renewals, health records, and property transactions can help to streamline the delivery of these services and make them more accessible to all citizens.

Amsterdam, Netherlands
Digital transformation programs in the city of Amsterdam have placed it as the world's leading smart city in many respects. Its dedicated approach to inclusive urban transformation has in many ways set it aside from all other smart cities. In collaboration with the global nonprofit innovation

firm, World Enabled, the city set out to develop new capabilities based on artificial intelligence, machine learning, and machine vision as part of its Amsterdam for All[3] project. These new tools will allow Amsterdam to audit the entire city through images, with computer algorithms that "see," "tag," "quantify," and "qualify" access barriers, curb cuts, and other assets. This technology will accelerate a more integrated approach to asset management and drive investments in infrastructure upgrading with a more nuanced approach. Layers of census data can be cross-referenced with identified access barriers and infrastructure improvements can consider access needs from the very beginning.

In addition to improving the accessibility of its urban infrastructure, Amsterdam is also using AI to improve the readability of its websites and make them more accessible to users with disabilities. This includes the use of machine vision to identify and tag elements on the website that may be difficult for users with visual impairments to access, such as small fonts or low contrast text.

Quito, Ecuador
One of the key aims of Quito's smart city initiatives is to increase the city's resilience in the face of natural disasters, such as earthquakes, floods, fires, and mudslides. To achieve this goal, Quito has introduced the "Quito Listo" program, which uses data and technology to help build a culture of prevention and awareness of risks in the city. The program uses digital maps and alerts to provide detailed information about the likelihood of significant structural damage and the areas of the city that are most at risk, such as those with large numbers of children or elderly people. This information can be used to target resources during emergencies and ensure that the most vulnerable members of the community are protected.

In addition to increasing resilience, Quito is also working to increase accessibility and innovation in the city through initiatives such as the development of green corridors and the National Inclusive Mobility Strategy. The green corridors are dedicated bike lanes and pedestrian pathways that are designed to improve mobility and reduce air pollution in the city, while the National Inclusive Mobility Strategy aims to increase accessibility and inclusivity in the city's transportation system.

---

[3] Amsterdam Intelligence, (2022). *Amsterdam for All Accessed 1 December 2022.* (https://amsterdamintelligence.com/projects/amsterdam-for-all). More recent publications by World Enabled and the City of Amsterdam such as the AI Playbook on Inclusive and Accessible Cities also elaborate on these emerging trends.

NEOM, Saudi Arabia

NEOM seeks to excel and radically expand the existing norms and notions of city building. This ambitious and visionary city is being built in the Tabuk Province in northwestern Saudi Arabia. It's billed as the world's first major development that will exceed all existing standards in environment protection, climate adaptation, net zero construction, digital transformation, and notably also accessibility. It proposes the large-scale development of futuristic urban environments including The Line, a 170 km long and 500 m tall continuous structure that will eventually accommodate 9 million people but built on a footprint of just 34 km^2 (Figs. 7.1 and 7.2).

The linear city faces considerable constraints. If and when completed, it will likely look substantially different than the original design. The project is set to be built on a physical and digital infrastructure layer while all essential utilities and transportation services will be integrated below the surface. This will mean a reduced infrastructure footprint, access to all necessary facilities within five minutes, and a high speed rail transport system with an end-to-end transit time of only 20 minutes. How this all comes together will is yet to be determined, the project is in a state of continual controversy and practical re-visioning and re-engineering.

Fig. 7.1 Mockup of the Line plan. This image shows a mirrored building that is long and tall but very narrow. The mirrored surface reflects the desert and water from the ocean. (Image credit: NEOM, (2022) *NEOM. Accessed November 30, 2022.* (https://www.neom.com/en-us/regions/theline))

Fig. 7.2 Design concepts for The Line project (NEOM, (2022) *NEOM. Accessed November 30, 2022.* (https://www.neom.com/en-us/regions/theline)). Digital mockup of the Line Project, this image shows abundant greenery with walking and swimming areas within an urban construction

The project has been plagued by challenges, but yet in all conversations with leaders, there is a clear interest to operationalize and exceed standards on accessibility and inclusion. The questions that remain are how will accessibility and inclusion be managed, planned for, budgeted, implemented and ultimately reviewed? What procedures and quality controls have been put in place? How can this city of the future deliver on access and sustainability of residents today? How will competing interests be reconciled and delivered? Can all systems be brought on board at the same time? It's going to take new approaches, new thinking, and a new operating system to deliver accessibility and sustainability simultaneously. Essentially project partners seek to provide a new blueprint for the future. The most telling elements of NEOM will be in the lessons learned, the potential to establish new approaches, and innovations that center inclusion and accessibility in city building on a mass scale.

What Can We Learn From These Cities?

The efforts of cities globally to create dynamic, vibrant, and inclusive smart cities, including the cities outlined above, are vital in furthering the creation of accessible designs, environments, and cultures. What makes these types of initiatives even more important is that they help to foster a culture of "a race to the top." Each approach benefits the inhabitants of those urban environments but also acts as an example to other cities around the world of what is possible and what should become the new norms for leading international cities.

These types of initiatives have the potential to transform urban planning and create more sustainable and resilient communities. The success of these initiatives will depend on the ability of cities to effectively adopt and integrate these technologies in a way that supports the needs of all citizens and promotes inclusivity and accessibility. But by building inclusion and access into their city-wide master plans, countries are taking the necessary steps to becoming Smart Nations. These are nations that embrace the capabilities and possibilities of new technologies and new approaches, as well as the capabilities and potential of all of their citizens.

Emerging Trends Linking Radical Inclusion to Resilience in Practice

There are several measures that can be put into practice to implement radical inclusion so as to boost the urban resilience of our cities. The following are some particularly compelling examples that can be used as a starting point:

- Human-rights based regulatory frameworks: Clear human-rights based regulatory frameworks can ensure that technologies do not reinforce exclusion, discrimination, or power asymmetries.
- Agile regulatory structures: Governments can issue agile regulatory structures that specify standards and guidelines for the accessibility and usability of digital products and services, such as apps, websites, and kiosks, to ensure that all citizens have equal access to these resources.
- Protection of citizens: Governments, both local and national, should protect citizens, including those with disabilities and vulnerable people, when collecting and using data for technology development.
- Collaboration with civil society organizations: Emerging technologies can maximize benefits and minimize harm by collaborating with civil society organizations, academia, policymakers, and disability rights organizations (DPOs).

- Monitoring and assessment: Local governments can monitor and assess the impact of emerging technologies on citizens, particularly those with disabilities and those at risk of exclusion, to ensure that these technologies are not reinforcing exclusion, discrimination, or power asymmetries.
- Risk management plans: Local governments can create risk management plans to increase their cyber inclusion and resilience by guaranteeing the delivery of essential city services.
- Continuous learning, training, and upskilling: All urban stakeholders, especially those driving policy or investment decisions, should allocate budgets for training, learning, and development programs. Upskilling allows new approaches to be systematized, calibrated, and implemented by a capable and engaged workforce.

In addition to the above, cities that are committed to radical inclusion can utilize Universal Design principles to enhance the effectiveness of their efforts.[4] The practice of Universal Design has expanded greatly from its origins in architecture to include policy, social participation, and health and wellness. The emerging measures presented in this book build off of Universal Design to help urban practitioners build belonging by design. How can we define the outcomes of radical inclusion in ways that can be measured and applied to all design domains? How can we do so while taking into account existing resources? Can we consider functional, social, and emotional dimensions? How can we enhance and support the creation of an interdisciplinary knowledge base for radical inclusion? We see the seeds of this already happening. Distinct fields such as anthropometrics, biomechanics, perception, cognition, safety, health promotion, and social interaction are increasingly overlapping and creating new expectations for designers, planners, and policymakers. In addition, urban planners, engineers, architects, and other stakeholders are already using these goals to guide their practice.

Cities that are committed to radical inclusion are already putting radically inclusive approaches into practice. One way cities are doing this is by developing peer-to-peer learning communities and participating in global networks such as the Cities for All Global Network on Inclusive and Accessible Urban Development (IAUD) or the The Empowered Cities

---

[4] Steinfeld, E. and Maisel, J., (2012). *Universal Design: Creating inclusive environments.* John Wiley & Sons.

network.[5] There are a variety of specific ways that cities committed to inclusive innovation and radical inclusion are creating peer-to-peer learning programs or actively learning from each other:

1. Hosting or participating in conferences or workshops: Cities are hosting or participating in conferences or workshops focused on inclusive innovation and radical inclusion, where city leaders are learning from each other and sharing best practices and challenges.
2. Joining or creating a network or forum: Cities are participating in networks or forums specifically focused on inclusive innovation and radical inclusion. This is being done through online platforms or in-person meetings and provides a space for ongoing communication and exchange among city leaders.
3. Engaging in mutual learning and exchange through partnerships and exchanges with other cities: These partnerships or exchanges involve technical assistance, policy sharing, and knowledge exchange and are focused on inclusive innovation and radical inclusion.
4. Using social media and online platforms to connect and share: Cities are connecting online with other cities and sharing information and best practices related to inclusive innovation and radical inclusion. This includes creating online communities or groups, using hashtags to share information and engaging in online discussions with other city leaders.
5. Partnering with organizations or networks in other cities that facilitate peer-to-peer learning and exchange: These partnerships are providing access to a range of resources and expertise, as well as the opportunity to connect with other cities that are also committed to inclusive innovation and radical inclusion.

A practical example for the points above has already been put to practice through a unique partnership between United Cities and Local Governments, Pineda Foundation/World Enabled, the World Blind Union, and other partners. The most impactful elements, including setting up of learning communities during the pandemic and a community of

---

[5] These networks to some degree overlap and include the cities of New York, Boston, Los Angeles, San Francisco, and Chicago, and many others. They work across key areas including employment, financial empowerment, and housing. These types of networks are vital in ensuring that cities can coordinate their work with and for people with disabilities. Networks also serve a key role in facilitating communication and exchange between city leaders and decision makers in other cities.

practice, focused on inclusive and accessible cities. Global and regional Cities for All communities helped promote peer-to-peer learning opportunities and accelerate the adoption of emerging standards.

In summary, there are many ways that cities can support radical inclusion, including setting up peer-to-peer learning programs, utilizing Universal Design goals, and participating in global networks. Technology can help with all of these measures. It is important to keep these efforts focused on radical inclusion and to ensure that they are inclusive and accessible to all.

Pop Up Box: How Can We Finance Inclusive Urban Transformation?

Financing of inclusive infrastructure requires creative and unconventional approaches that align interests and partnership for sustainable and lasting impact. Below are four sources of funding that ideally should work together:

Governments: Local, regional, and national governments can provide funding for urban transformation efforts through various mechanisms, such as grants, loans, or tax incentives.
Private sector: Private companies, foundations, and other organizations can also provide funding for urban transformation efforts, either through direct investment or through partnerships with governments or other organizations.
International organizations: International organizations such as the United Nations or the World Bank can provide funding for urban transformation efforts through grants, loans, or other forms of financial assistance.
Community groups and nonprofit organizations: Community groups and nonprofit organizations can also play a role in financing urban transformation efforts, either through fundraising or by leveraging their own resources.

Ultimately, the financing for urban transformation efforts may be shared by multiple sources, and the specific distribution of funding will depend on the specific goals and needs of the project, as well as the availability of resources. It is important to consider the long-term sustainability of financing sources and to ensure that funding is allocated in a fair and transparent manner.

Where Do We Go From Here?

Throughout this book we have explored the keys to inclusive and sustainable urban transformation. But what happens if we fail? What are the costs of inaction? How can we ensure city leaders and other urban stakeholders have the tools to act?

There are several vital elements that will help summarize all the insights gathered in the previous pages. To achieve radically inclusive and sustainable urban transformation the following key elements should be top of mind:

Accessibility: Ensuring that cities are physically and digitally accessible to people of all ages, abilities, and backgrounds is essential for promoting greater inclusion and participation. This can involve designing infrastructure and public spaces that are physically accessible, as well as implementing policies and technologies that support digital accessibility.

Affordability: Ensuring that cities are affordable for all residents, particularly those with low incomes or marginalized backgrounds, is crucial for promoting greater social and economic inclusion. This can involve implementing policies such as rent control or inclusionary zoning, as well as investing in affordable housing and other social infrastructure.

Inclusivity: Building inclusive cities requires considering the needs and perspectives of all residents and ensuring that policies and interventions are designed to support the full participation and belonging of all members of the community. This can involve implementing participatory planning processes and engaging diverse stakeholders in decision-making.

Sustainability: Ensuring that cities are environmentally sustainable is essential for building long-term resilience and addressing global challenges such as climate change. This can involve implementing green infrastructure, promoting sustainable transportation options, and adopting energy-efficient technologies.

If we get this wrong and fail to address these key ingredients, the implications can be significant. For example, if cities are not physically or digitally accessible, individuals with disabilities or other marginalized groups may face barriers to participating fully in society. If cities are not affordable, low-income residents may be forced to live in areas with limited access to opportunities, leading to social and economic exclusion. If cities are not inclusive, residents may feel disconnected from the community and may not have a voice in decision-making processes. And if cities are not sustainable, they may be less resilient to environmental and economic shocks and may contribute to global environmental challenges.

Cities Are Not Waiting on the Sidelines, They Are Leading the Charge for Radical Inclusion

Cities are not waiting for this transformation to take place, city leaders are taking charge. From Amsterdam to Abu Dhabi, from Belgrade to Boston, from Mersin to Medellin, there is a global movement building to accelerate an inclusive urban transformation. I have shared my insights and experiences witnessing and leading these efforts alongside visionary mayors and other civic leaders. Leaders like Emilia Saiz, the Secretary General of UCLG, or Ban Ki-Moon, the Secretary General of the UN, who understand that the future will be won or lost in cities. That it is up to each one of us to build a more inclusive, accessible, and resilient future.

But leaders are not waiting for a savior, real leadership is being put to the test each day. Cities are innovating on inclusion and are experimenting and putting in place new governance models to enhance resourcefulness, inclusivity, increase integration, and more.

To increase resourcefulness, cities as diverse as Quito and Amsterdam are adopting a creative and innovative approach to using their resources. This involves identifying new sources of funding and support, such as partnerships with businesses and organizations, and exploring alternative financing mechanisms, such as crowdfunding or social impact bonds. Cities are also looking for opportunities to share resources and services with other municipalities in order to reduce costs and increase efficiency, all while prioritizing the theme of radical inclusion and belonging.

To enhance inclusivity, cities like Abu Dhabi are prioritizing broad consultation and involving a diverse range of stakeholders in decision-making. Cities are establishing advisory committees or task forces that bring together representatives from different sectors and communities and providing a platform for them to share their perspectives and ideas. Cities like Barcelona are also using digital tools and platforms, such as online forums and social media, to engage with a wider range of citizens and stakeholders, all while weaving in the themes of radical inclusion and belonging.

To increase integration, cities like New York are working to foster collaboration and coordination among different systems and institutions. This involves establishing interagency agreements and partnerships and creating mechanisms for sharing information and resources. Cities like

Chicago are also developing and implementing city-wide plans and strategies that take into account the needs and priorities of all sectors and stakeholders, all while promoting the themes of radical inclusion and belonging.

To increase robustness, cities like Los Angeles are focusing on designing and implementing well-conceived, constructed, and managed systems. This involves investing in infrastructure and services that are resilient to natural disasters and other disruptions and adopting best practices in project management and risk assessment. Cities like London and Doha are also establishing clear policies and procedures for asset management. They are tracking and monitoring costs associated with maintaining and upgrading their systems over time, all while prioritizing the themes of radical inclusion and belonging.

To increase redundancy, cities like Bogota and Berkeley are creating spare capacity in their systems and infrastructure in order to accommodate disruption. This involves designing buildings and infrastructure with multiple redundant systems or establishing backup power sources and other contingency plans. Cities are also investing in technologies and systems that are scalable and flexible, in order to adapt to changing circumstances and demands, all while promoting the themes of radical inclusion and belonging.

These are all emerging and quickly proving to be the new norm. However, to truly understand these transformations, we will need to also have integrated and coordinated research efforts: Research that supports the scaling up of evidence based policies, research that helps drive funding to effective programs.

Some potential research questions that could guide future research on radically inclusive and sustainable urban transformation, with a focus on technology and innovation as a cross-cutting theme, include:

1. How can technology and innovation be leveraged to design cities that are physically and digitally accessible to people of all ages, abilities, and backgrounds?
2. What policies and interventions can be implemented to ensure that cities are affordable for all residents, particularly those with low incomes or marginalized backgrounds, and how can technology and innovation support these efforts?
3. How can we use technology and innovation to engage diverse stakeholders in decision-making processes and ensure that policies and

interventions are inclusive and responsive to the needs of all members of the community?
4. What role can technology and innovation play in promoting sustainability and environmental resilience in cities, and how can these strategies be balanced with the needs and priorities of all residents?
5. How can we use technology and innovation to measure and evaluate the impact of inclusive and sustainable urban transformation efforts, and how can we use this information to inform future interventions and policies?
6. How can technology and innovation be used to identify and address the unique challenges and needs of different marginalized or excluded groups in the context of urban transformation, and how can we ensure that these groups are fully included and supported?
7. What are the best practices and lessons learned from successful urban transformation efforts that have incorporated technology and innovation, and how can these be replicated and scaled in other cities?

In conclusion, it is clear that creating cities of tomorrow that prioritize inclusion and belonging requires a holistic and collaborative approach. An approach that understands the emergence of new technologies but does not depend on them, but rather centers on human values and meaningful governance systems. Each chapter of this book has highlighted the importance of considering the implications of these topics at every stage of development, from project planning to execution and monitoring. It is vital that various stakeholders work together to develop radically different and inclusive approaches that center the needs and experiences of all members of the community.

Moreover, it is essential that inclusion and belonging are integral components of a new and emerging governance process. This means ensuring that the voices and perspectives of marginalized groups are actively sought out and considered in decision-making processes. It also means taking a proactive approach to addressing issues of inequality and discrimination, rather than simply reacting to problems as they arise.

Overall, the key learnings from this book demonstrate the urgent need for cities to prioritize inclusion and belonging in order to create truly sustainable and equitable communities. By adopting a unified and holistic approach, we can build cities that foster a sense of belonging for all residents and create a more inclusive and just society for all. It is up to each one of us to build a new blueprint for cities, one based on inclusivity, collaboration, and a deeply authentic resonance with emerging social knowledge and wisdom. Above all, we must build the future we need with love and joy for our all our children, and as indigenous communities teach, an additional seven generations yet to come.

References

Amsterdam Intelligence. (n.d.). *Amsterdam for All*. Retrieved December 1, 2022, from https://amsterdamintelligence.com/projects/amsterdam-for-all

Cheshmehzangi, A. (2020). *The City in Need: Urban Resilience and City Management in Disruptive Disease Outbreak Events*. Springer. https://doi.org/10.1007/978-981-15-5487-2

NEOM. (n.d.). *THE LINE: a revolution in urban living*. Retrieved May 19, 2023, from https://www.neom.com/en-us/regions/theline

Pineda, V. (2020, August 16). Resilience and Recovery Strategies for People with Disabilities in Response to a Pandemic | LinkedIn. *LinkedIn*. https://www.linkedin.com/pulse/resilience-recovery-strategies-people-disabilities-response-pineda/

Steinfeld, E., & Maisel, J. (2012). *Universal design: Creating inclusive environments*. John Wiley & Sons.

UN Habitat. (n.d.). *Capacity Building*. http://capacitybuildingunhabitat.org/about-capacity-building/

Open Access This chapter is licensed under the terms of the Creative Commons Attribution 4.0 International License (http://creativecommons.org/licenses/by/4.0/), which permits use, sharing, adaptation, distribution and reproduction in any medium or format, as long as you give appropriate credit to the original author(s) and the source, provide a link to the Creative Commons licence and indicate if changes were made.

The images or other third party material in this chapter are included in the chapter's Creative Commons licence, unless indicated otherwise in a credit line to the material. If material is not included in the chapter's Creative Commons licence and your intended use is not permitted by statutory regulation or exceeds the permitted use, you will need to obtain permission directly from the copyright holder.

References

Agarwal, P. (2020, April 12). What neuroimaging can tell us about our unconscious biases. *Scientific American.* https://blogs.scientificamerican.com/observations/what-neuroimaging-can-tell-us-about-our-unconscious-biases/

American Planning Association. (n.d.). *Social Equity.* Knowledgebase Collection. https://www.planning.org/knowledgebase/equity/

Anderson, J., Rainie, L., & Vogels, E. A. (2021, February 18). Experts say the "new normal" in 2025 will be far more tech-driven, presenting more big challenges. *PEW Research Center.* https://www.pewresearch.org/internet/2021/02/18/experts-say-the-new-normal-in-2025-will-be-far-more-tech-driven-presenting-more-big-challenges/

Albarracín, D., Zanna, M. P., Johnson, B. T., & Kumakale, G. T. (2005). Attitudes: Introduction and scope. In D. Albarracín, B. T. Johnson, & M. P. Zanna (Eds.), *The Handbook of Attitudes* (pp. 3–20). Lawrence Erlbaum Associates Publishers.

Amsterdam Intelligence. (n.d.). *Amsterdam for All.* Retrieved December 1, 2022, from https://amsterdamintelligence.com/projects/amsterdam-for-all

Armendaris, F. (2015). *World Inclusive Cities Approach Paper* (No. AUS8539). World Bank Group. https://documents1.worldbank.org/curated/en/402451468169453117/pdf/AUS8539-REVISED-WP-P148654-PUBLIC-Box393236B-Inclusive-Cities-Approach-Paper-w-Annexes-final.pdf

Baumgartner, F. R., Jones, B. D., & Mortensen, P. B. (2018). Punctuated equilibrium theory: Explaining stability and change in public policymaking. *Theories of the Policy Process,* 55–101.

Beasley, V. B. (2020). The Trouble with Marching: Ableism, Visibility, and Exclusion of People with Disabilities. *Rhetoric Society Quarterly, 50*(3), 166–174. https://doi.org/10.1080/02773945.2020.1752127

Bergou, N., Hammoud, R., Smythe, M., Gibbons, J., Davidson, N., Tognin, S., Reeves, G., Shepherd, J., & Mechelli, A. (2022). The mental health benefits of visiting canals and rivers: An ecological momentary assessment study. *Plos One, 17*(8), e0271306. https://doi.org/10.1371/journal.pone.0271306

Buckup, S. (2009). *The price of exclusion: The economic consequences of excluding people with disabilities from the world of work*. International Labour Organization.

Burning Man Project. (n.d.). *The 10 Principles of Burning Man*. https://burningman.org/culture/philosophical-center/

CBM. (n.d.). *The Inclusion Imperative: Towards Disability-inclusive and Accessible Urban Development*. Disability Inclusive and Accessible Urban Development Network. https://www.cbm.org/fileadmin/user_upload/Publications/The-Inclusion-Imperative-Towards-Disability-Inclusive-and-Accessible-Urb....pdf

Chan, Kok Hui, J. (2020, September 3). Rebuilding cities better in the post-COVID-19 world. *Asia Global Institute*. https://www.asiaglobalonline.hku.hk/rebuilding-cities-better-post-covid-19-world

Chen, B., & McNamara, D. M. (2020). Disability discrimination, medical rationing and COVID-19. *Asian Bioethics Review, 12*(4), 511–518. https://www.ncbi.nlm.nih.gov/pmc/articles/PMC7471485/

Chen, Z. (2019). Grand Challenges in Construction Management. *Frontiers in Built Environment, 5*. https://doi.org/10.3389/fbuil.2019.00031

Cheshmehzangi, A. (2020). *The City in Need: Urban Resilience and City Management in Disruptive Disease Outbreak Events*. Springer. https://doi.org/10.1007/978-981-15-5487-2

Chenier, E. (2020). *Radical Inclusion: Equity and Diversity Among Female Faculty at Simon Fraser University*. Academic Women of SFU. https://www2.unbc.ca/sites/default/files/sections/equity-diversity-inclusion/radicalinclusion-aug312020.pdf

Cities for All Training Program. (2020, November 27). *Module Two: Non-Discrimination*. https://cities4all.org/wp-content/uploads/2020/12/C4A-Training-Program-Modules-2-Final.pdf

Fagence, M. (1977). *Citizen Participation in Planning*. Pergamon Press.

Farazmand, A. (2009). Building administrative capacity for the age of rapid globalization: A modest prescription for the twenty-first century. *Public Administration Review, 69*(6), 1007–1020.

Ferrari, L., Berlingerio, M., Calabrese, F., & Reades, J. (2014). Improving the accessibility of urban transportation networks for people with disabilities. *Transportation Research Part C: Emerging Technologies, 45*, 27–40.

Fleischer, D. Z., & Zames, F. (2011). *The Disability Rights Movement: From charity to confrontation*. Temple University Press. http://www.jstor.org/stable/j.ctt14bt7kv

Forester, J. (1993). *Critical theory, public policy, and planning practice*. State University of New York Press.

Frey, W. H. (2021). Pandemic population change across metro America: Accelerated migration, less immigration, fewer births and more deaths. *Brookings.* https://www.brookings.edu/research/pandemic-population-change-across-metro-america-accelerated-migration-less-immigration-fewer-births-and-more-deaths/

Froehlich, J. E., Eisenberg, Y., Hosseini, M., Miranda, F., Adams, M., Caspi, A., Dieterich, H., Feldner, H., Gonzalez, A., & De Gyves, C. (2022). The Future of Urban Accessibility for People with Disabilities: Data Collection, Analytics, Policy, and Tools. *Proceedings of the 24th International ACM SIGACCESS Conference on Computers and Accessibility,* 1–8.

Georgetown University National Center for Cultural Competence. (n.d.). *Conscious & Unconscious Biases in Health Care.* https://nccc.georgetown.edu/bias/module-3/4.php

Global Future Council on Cities and Urbanization. (2018, September). *Agile Cities: Preparing for the Fourth Industrial Revolution.* World Economic Forum. Retrieved May 20, 2023, from https://www.weforum.org/whitepapers/agile-cities-preparing-for-the-fourth-industrial-revolution/

Golby, A. J., Gabrieli, J. D. E., Chiao, J. Y., & Eberhardt, J. L. (2001). Differential responses in the fusiform region to same-race and other-race faces. *Nature Publishing Group.* https://web.stanford.edu/~eberhard/downloads/200108-DifferentialResponses.pdf

Graham, G., Ostrowski, M., & Sabina, A. (2015, August 6). Defeating the ZIP code health paradigm: Data, technology, and collaboration are key. *Health Affairs.* https://www.healthaffairs.org/do/10.1377/forefront.20150806.049730

Gould, E., & Shierholtz, H. (2020, March 19). Not everybody can work from home: Black and Hispanic workers are much less likely to be able to telework. *Economic Policy Institute.* Retrieved May 17, 2023, from https://www.epi.org/blog/black-and-hispanic-workers-are-much-less-likely-to-be-able-to-work-from-home/

Guzman, L. A., Oviedo, D., & Rivera, C. (2017). Assessing equity in transport accessibility to work and study: The Bogotá region. *Journal of Transport Geography, 58,* 236–246.

HABITAT III. (2015). *HABITAT III ISSUE PAPERS 1 – INCLUSIVE CITIES.* United Nations. https://uploads.habitat3.org/hb3/Habitat-III-Issue-Paper-1_Inclusive-Cities-2.0.pdf

Habitat III. (n.d.-a). *Habitat III.* Retrieved May 19, 2023, from https://habitat3.org

Habitat III. (n.d.-b). *Issue Papers.* Retrieved May 19, 2023, from https://habitat3.org/documents-and-archive/preparatory-documents/issue-papers/

Harris, R. (2021). *How Cities Matter.* Cambridge University Press.

Harvey, D. (1973). *Social Justice and the City.* University of Georgia Press.

Holmes, K. (2018). *Mismatch: How inclusion shapes design*. MIT Press.
Huang, X., White, M., & Langenheim, N. (2022). Towards an Inclusive Walking Community—A Multi-Criteria Digital Evaluation Approach to Facilitate Accessible Journeys. *Buildings*, *12*(8), 1191. https://doi.org/10.3390/buildings12081191
Ionescu, D. (2022, November 15). Why Accessible Sidewalks Fall by the Wayside. *Planetizen*. https://www.planetizen.com/news/2022/11/119678-why-accessible-sidewalks-fall-wayside
Kempin Reuter, T. (2019). Human rights and the city: Including marginalized communities in urban development and smart cities. *Journal of Human Rights*, *18*(4), 382–402.
Kratochwil, F. V. (1991). *Rules, norms, and decisions: On the conditions of practical and legal reasoning in international relations and domestic affairs*. Cambridge University Press.
Kristof, N. (2015, May 7). Our Biased Brains. *New York Times*. https://www.nytimes.com/2015/05/07/opinion/nicholas-kristof-our-biased-brains.html
Lefebvre, H. (1998). *The Right to the City*.
Lefebvre, H., Kofman, E., & Lebas, E. (1996). *Writings on Cities*. Blackwell Oxford.
Libertun de Duren, N., Salazar, J. P., Duryea, S., Mastellaro, C., Freeman, L., Pedraza, L., Rodriguez Porcel, M., Sandoval, D., Aguerre, J. A., & Angius, C. (2021). *Cities as spaces for opportunities for all: Building public spaces for people with disabilities, children and elders*.
Lifchez, R., & Winslow, B. (1981). *Design for independent living: The environment and physically disabled people*. University of California Press.
Mercille, J. (2021). Inclusive smart cities: beyond voluntary corporate data sharing. *Sustainability*, *13*(15), 8135.
Mishra, P. & Gowda, B. (2022, November 11). RampMyCity, a startup making cities more able for the disabled. *The Hindu*. https://www.thehindu.com/news/cities/bangalore/rampmycity-this-startup-making-cities-more-able-for-the-disabled/article66125754.ece
Mitra, S. (2006). The Capability Approach and Disability. *Journal of Disability Policy Studies 16*(4), 236–247.
Mollaoglu, S., Sparkling, A., & Thomas, S. (2015). An inquiry to move an underutilized best practice forward: Barriers to partnering in the architecture, engineering, and construction industry. *Project Management Journal*, *46*(1), 69–83.
NEOM. (n.d.). *THE LINE: a revolution in urban living*. Retrieved May 19, 2023, from https://www.neom.com/en-us/regions/theline
Nussbaum, M. C. (2007). Frontiers of Justice: Disability, Nationality, Species Membership. Harvard University Press. https://doi.org/10.4159/9780674041578

Othering & Belonging Institute. (2017, February 8). *Targeted Universalism: Animated Video*. Retrieved May 20, 2023, from https://belonging.berkeley.edu/targeted-universalism-animated-video

Othering and Belonging Institute. (n.d.). *Home*. Retrieved May 19, 2023, from https://belonging.berkeley.edu/

Othering and Belonging Institute. (2019). *New primer: Targeted universalism opens pathways for policy innovation*. https://belonging.berkeley.edu/tu-press-release

Phelps, E. A., O'Connor, K. J., Cunningham, W. A., Funayama, E. S., Gatenby, J. C., Gore, J. C., & Banaji, M. R. (2000). Performance on Indirect Measures of Race Evaluation Predicts Amygdala Activation. *Journal of Cognitive Neuroscience*, *12*(5), 729–738. https://doi.org/10.1162/089892900562552

Piepzna-Samarasinha, L. L. (2018). *Care work: Dreaming disability justice*. Arsenal Pulp Press.

Pineda, V. S. (2008). Enabling justice: Spatializing disability in the built environment. *Critical Planning Journal*, *15*, 111–123.

Pineda, V. (2016, August 22). Building a City of Radical Inclusion. *Hostfully*. https://travel.hostfully.com/building-a-city-of-radical-inclusion-d14ba7e1aa0f

Pineda, V. (2020a). *Building the inclusive city: governance, access, and the urban transformation of Dubai*. Springer Nature.

Pineda, V. (2020b, August 16). Resilience and Recovery Strategies for People with Disabilities in Response to a Pandemic | LinkedIn. *LinkedIn*. https://www.linkedin.com/pulse/resilience-recovery-strategies-people-disabilities-response-pineda/

Pineda, V. (n.d.). Webinar 4: Age-Friendly Cities. *Combined Accessibility Blogs*.

Pineda, V. S., & Corburn, J. (2020). Disability, urban health equity, and the coronavirus pandemic: promoting cities for all. *Journal of Urban Health*, *97*, 336–341.

Pineda, V. S., Meyer, S., & Cruz, J. P. (2017). The inclusion imperative. Forging an inclusive new urban agenda. *The Journal of Public Space*, *2*(4), 1–20.

powell, john a., Ake, W., & Menendian, S. (2019). *Targeted Universalism: Policy & Practice*. https://escholarship.org/uc/item/9sm8b0q8

powell, john a. (2020). Post-Racialism or Targeted Universalism. *Denver Law Review*, *86*(3).

Prince, M. J. (2008). Inclusive City Life: Persons with Disabilities and the Politics of Difference. *Society for Disability Studies*, *2008*(1). https://dsq-sds.org/article/view/65/65

Rawls, J. (1971). *A Theory of Justice*. Belknap Press.

Rawls, J. (1958). Justice as Fairness. *The Philosophical Review*, *67*(2), 164–194.

Ricci, L. (2022). Integrated Approaches to Ecosystem Services: Linking Culture, Circular Economy and Environment through the Re-Use of Open Spaces and Buildings in Europe. *Land*, *11*(8), 1161.

Rico, I. V. (2021). Smart cities for all: usability and disability bias. *European Review of Digital Administration and Law*, *2*(1), 157.

Rothstein, R. (2017). *The Color of Law: A forgotten history of how our government segregated America*. Liveright Publishing.

Schwab, K. (2016). *The Fourth Industrial Revolution*. World Economic Forum. https://law.unimelb.edu.au/__data/assets/pdf_file/0005/3385454/Schwab-The_Fourth_Industrial_Revolution_Klaus_S.pdf

Schweik, S. M. (2010). *The Ugly Laws: Disability in public*. NYU Press.

Sen, A. (1999). *Commodities and capabilities*. Oxford University Press.

Shapiro, J. (2020, December 14). As hospital fear being overwhelmed by COVID-19, do the disabled get the same access? *National Public Radio*. https://www.npr.org/2020/12/14/945056176/as-hospitals-fear-being-overwhelmed-by-covid-19-do-the-disabled-get-the-same-acc

Singru, R. N. (2021, April 8). The digital transformation caused by the pandemic can be a powerful tool for inclusive city planning. *Asian Development Blog*. https://blogs.adb.org/blog/digital-transformation-caused-pandemic-can-be-powerful-tool-inclusive-city-planning

Soja, E. W. (2009). The City and Spatial Justice. *Spatial Justice*. https://www.jssj.org/wp-content/uploads/2012/12/JSSJ1-1en4.pdf

Soja, E. W. (2013). *Seeking Spatial Justice*. University of Minnesota Press.

Steinfeld, E., & Maisel, J. (2012). *Universal design: Creating inclusive environments*. John Wiley & Sons.

United Nations, Department of Economic and Social Affairs. (2017). *World Population Aging 2017 – Highlights*. https://www.un.org/en/development/desa/population/publications/pdf/ageing/WPA2017_Highlights.pdf

United Nations, Department of Economic and Social Affairs, Population Division. (2018). *2018 Revision of the World Urbanization Prospects*. https://esa.un.org/unpd/wup/

United Nations. (2019). *Disability and Development Report. Realizing the Sustainable Development Goals by, for and with Persons with Disabilities 2018*. United Nations, Department of Economic and Social Affairs.

UN Habitat. (n.d.). *Capacity Building*. http://capacitybuildingunhabitat.org/about-capacity-building/

University of California Television (UCTV). (2008, January 31). *Martha Nussbaum – Conversations with History*. https://www.youtube.com/watch?v=Qy3YTzYjut4

Wildavsky, A. B. (1986). *Budgeting: A comparative theory of the budgeting process*. Transaction Publishers.

World Economic Forum. (2016). *Shaping the Future of Construction: A Breakthrough in Mindset and Technology*. Retrieved May 16, 2023, from https://www.weforum.org/reports/shaping-the-future-of-construction-a-breakthrough-in-mindset-and-technology/

World Health Organization. (2018, May 18). *Assistive Technology*. Assistive Technology. https://www.who.int/news-room/fact-sheets/detail/assistive-technology

World Health Organization & World Bank. (2011). *World Report on Disability* (No. 978-92-4-156418-2). https://www.who.int/publications/i/item/9789241564182

Young, I. M. (2011). *Justice and the Politics of Difference*. Princeton University Press.

Index[1]

A

Able-bodied person, 48
Ableism, vi, 50
Abnormality, 43
Access, vii, ix, 4, 6, 7, 9, 10, 13n20, 15, 20, 26, 26n3, 28, 30, 31, 34, 44, 46, 52, 53, 56, 57, 64–66, 69–74, 71n11, 76, 78–82, 86, 87, 95, 99, 100, 102–108, 112, 116, 117, 120, 121, 124, 125, 136, 138, 139, 141–144, 146, 148
Accessibility, vi–viii, 8, 11, 14, 20, 40n1, 48, 55, 57, 67–70, 73, 74, 76, 79–82, 87, 94, 99, 101–104, 106–108, 112, 117, 120, 120n7, 122, 126, 130, 137, 139–144, 148
  improvements, 11, 36
  standards, 3, 102, 104, 125
Accessible cities, 19, 76, 106, 108, 137–144, 147
Accessible design standards, 102
Accessible locations, 35
Accessible mental health services, 35
Accessible networks, 36
Accessible sidewalks, 36, 139
Accessible spaces, viii, x, 79, 118, 126
Accessible transportation, 138
Accountability, ix, 55, 100, 101, 122
Active aging, 96
Active transportation, 34, 35
Activism, 41, 42
Activists, 36, 40n1, 40n2, 126
Addicted to alcohol, 29
Administrative and coordinating capacity, 88, 91
Advocacy, 75, 121
Advocates, 14, 36, 40n1, 43, 44, 51, 73, 76, 98
Affordable housing, 4, 6, 100, 121, 128, 148
Age-accessible transportation, 97
Age-friendly cities, 96, 97
Ageism, 96
Agile regulatory structures, 144
Aging demographic trends, 3

---

[1] Note: Page numbers followed by 'n' refer to notes.

Aging population, 4, 12
Almshouse, 28
Americans With Disabilities Act, 20, 36, 76n18
Amsterdam, 78, 140–141, 149
Amsterdam for All project, 141
Amygdala, 45
Anthropometrics, 145
Anti freak bill, 27–28
Anti-discrimination policies, 54
Antifragile commodities or services, 13
Anxiety, 15, 34
Apartheid, 25, 65n6
Architects, 6, 32n8, 107, 118, 125, 126, 128, 145
Architecture, 25, 28, 32n8, 104, 125, 125n9, 126, 128, 145
Artificial Intelligence (AI), x, 112, 119, 120, 122, 123, 127, 128, 140, 141
Assistive communication devices, 33
Assistive technologies, 4, 140
Asylums, 28, 29
Attitudes, viii, 6, 27, 47, 81, 88–90, 92–94, 122
  towards the targeted group, 88
Attitudinal barriers, 51
Auditory distractions, 32
Augmented Reality (AR), 34, 120
Autism, 118, 120
Autism friendly cities, 31–33, 35
Autism friendly hotel, 33
Autonomous vehicles, 112, 119, 140
Awareness, 33, 48, 81, 93, 108, 117, 121, 141

Basic civil right, 36
Basic freedoms, 94, 95
Basic functionings, 94, 95
Beautiful cities, 28
Beautiful spaces, 19
Beliefs, 26, 27, 31, 44, 46, 56, 89, 92, 93
Bell curve, 12
Belonging, x, xiii, xiv, 5, 5n13, 8, 12, 15, 19, 20, 26, 40, 41, 65, 66, 86–88, 95, 113, 115, 118, 129, 135, 145, 148–151
  by design, ix, 73–76
Benchmark inclusion, 94
Berkeley, viin8, 40–43, 40n1, 40n2, 86, 114
Best practices, xiv, 11, 32, 46, 69, 70, 80, 112, 125n9, 136, 146, 150, 151
Biases, xiv, 6, 26, 44–46, 93, 127, 129
Big Data, 122, 124
Bike lanes, 20, 34, 141
Bike shares, 42, 42n9
Bike-sharing programs, 34, 123
Biomechanics, 145
Bioswales, 15, 15n23
Blackout curtains, 33
Blind colleges, 29
Blockchain, x, 119, 119n6, 121, 140
Blue corridors, 15, 17, 19
Blue spaces, 15–19, 34
Broad consultation, 134, 135, 149
Built environments, vi, viii, 5, 6, 8, 25, 27, 30, 31, 53, 63, 67, 73, 96, 101–102
Burning Man, 2, 48, 49, 87

B
Baltimore, 36
Barcelona, viin8, 78, 139, 149
Barrier-free society, 105
Barriers, v, vi, 2–7, 3n1, 25, 26, 30, 31, 48, 49, 51–55, 64, 66, 68, 74, 76n18, 86, 92, 107, 141, 148

C
Capabilities, viii, x, 4–8, 11, 13, 26n3, 42, 46, 47, 50, 52, 55, 64, 65, 80–82, 94, 101, 119, 126, 127, 136, 141, 144
  approach, 5n10, 6, 26n3
  deprivation, 5, 5n9, 64

Capability Model, 5
Capable, 13, 27, 31, 65n7, 101, 134, 145
Capacity building, 56, 75, 106, 126
Case study, xiv, 33, 87, 104–107, 118
Cebu city, 100
Cemeteries, 29
Charity Organization Society, 27
Chenier, Ele, 48
Cheonggyecheon Stream, 17–19
Chicago, 27, 71, 77, 146n5, 150
Chicago Riverwalk, 17
Cities of tomorrow, ix, 26, 49, 65, 66, 87, 112–130, 151
Citizenship, 26, 30, 46
City Beautiful movement, 28
City blocks, 30
City leader, xiv, 11, 26, 31, 53, 63, 65, 73, 80, 88, 101, 135, 146, 146n5, 148, 149
City structures, 30
Civil right, 36
Civil unrest, 31
Clear signage, 33
Climate change, 12–15, 34n9, 41, 66, 70, 75, 80, 124, 148
 adaptation, 13–14
Climate resilience, 103–104
Coalitions, 14, 42, 107, 108
Co-creating, 12
Collaboration, vii, 20, 93, 94, 105, 113, 125, 134, 135, 140, 144, 149
Columbus, 27
Commercial interests, 26
Commodifying, 28
Community-based organizations, 35
Community belonging, 19
Community Development Authority, 107
Community meetings, 35, 135
Community members, 14, 26, 113
Community of practice, 146
Community ownership, 15
Community participation, 49
Compliance, 36
Comprehensive approach, 34
Conducting outreach, 14
Construction companies, 6, 128
Construction industry, 11, 67–70, 125, 125n9
Construction management, 67, 68, 70, 128
Convalescent homes, 29
Convention on the Rights of Persons with Disabilities (CRPD), vii, 3n1, 105–107
Cost-effective process, 19
Cost saving measure, 11, 69
COVID-19 pandemic, 3, 49, 71, 75, 77, 78, 80, 136–139
Crip camp, 40n1, 43
Critical legal theory, 88
Crowdfunding, 117, 135, 149
Cuba, 42
Curb cuts, 6, 7, 9, 29, 30, 68, 141
Cyber inclusion, 145
Cycling, 34

D
Dangerous sidewalk conditions, 36
Data collection, xiv, 81, 88, 93, 122, 129, 130
Data management, 119n6, 122
Data, monitoring and evaluation, 56, 76, 101
Data privacy, 72, 136, 137
DeafSpace, 118
Deformed individuals, 28
Deformities, 28
Deira, 86
Denver, 27
Depression, 34

Design, vi–x, xiii, xiv, 2, 6–13, 9n17, 19, 20, 24–26, 29–35, 32n8, 43, 45n12, 47, 52, 53, 64, 67–69, 73–76, 78–80, 86–88, 95, 101–104, 106, 113, 114, 116–118, 123–125, 127–130, 143, 145, 150
  errors, 25
  standards, 67, 101–102, 118
Designers, 6, 9, 12, 113, 118, 127, 145
Designing environments, 31, 32n8
Developing partnerships, 14
Digital barriers, 3, 64
Digital infrastructure, 72, 107, 136, 142
Digital revolution, 118
Digital transformation, xiv, 12, 53, 70, 72, 75, 79, 107, 122, 134, 140, 142
Disabilities, vi–ix, xiii, 2–7, 3n1, 3n5, 4n6, 5n10, 9, 11, 11n18, 13–15, 13n20, 20, 25–31, 26n3, 36, 40, 40n1, 40n2, 43, 45–53, 50n17, 57, 64, 66, 67, 70, 71, 71n11, 73–82, 86, 87, 90, 92–94, 96–99, 102, 105–108, 113, 114n1, 115, 117, 118, 119n6, 120, 121, 123–125, 129, 137–141, 144, 145, 146n5, 148
  justice, 41, 49–52, 50n17
  rights, viii, 14, 40, 40n1, 40n2, 44, 49, 50n17, 99, 105, 121, 126, 144
  rights movement, 50, 50n17, 51
Disability-free boulevards, 28, 29
Disabled, vi, 3n1, 5, 24, 28, 30, 31, 40n2, 47, 48, 50–52, 50n17, 65, 74, 91, 92, 97, 99, 112, 125, 125n10, 126, 140
  people of color, 51
  women, 20

Disaster resilience and management, 136, 150
DisCo Policy Framework, x, 87–94
Discrimination, xiv, 6, 24, 25, 44, 45, 49, 50, 55, 56, 96, 122, 127, 129, 136, 144, 145, 151
Diseased, 27
Disempowerment, 5, 48
District of Columbia, 20
Diverse populations, 9n17, 19
Diversity, 2, 56, 105
  and inclusion, 86
Drainage, 28
Dubai, 86, 87, 104–107, 107n19, 119n6, 140
Dubai Disability Strategy, 86, 105–107, 140
Dubai Expo 2020, 107
Dubai Inclusive Education Policy Framework, 107
Dubai Municipality, 107
Dubai Universal Accessibility Strategy and Action Plan (DUASAP), 107
Dubai Universal Design Code, 107
Dwellers, 12, 31, 65

E
Economic exclusion, 6, 53
Economic marginalization, 31
Economic tensions, 31
Educating the public, 14
Education, 3, 6, 9n17, 24, 25, 40n1, 48, 64, 66, 70, 78, 81, 100, 105, 107, 123, 126, 138
Electronic revolution, 118
Emerging technologies, 113, 120, 121, 140, 144, 145
Emirate of Dubai, 107
Emotional brain, 45
Empowering people, 8, 13, 19, 96
Empowerment, 2, 56, 93, 146n5

Energy-efficient technologies, 148
Enforcing, 27
Engaging with the legal system, 14
Environmental inequity, 43
Environmental, Social, and Governance (ESG), 56
Environmental sustainability, 148
Epileptic farms, 28, 29
Equality, viii, ix, 2, 52, 53, 105, 116
Equitable, vi, x, xiii, 9, 30, 36, 53, 90, 105–107, 113, 121, 136, 138, 140, 151
    society, 41, 50, 51
    urban future, 67
Equity, vii, viin5, viin7, 2, 20, 31, 44, 53, 56, 65, 72n12, 80, 86, 87, 99, 105, 106, 115, 116, 137
Ethnic tensions, 31
Eugenic logic, 28
Eugenics, 28
Evaluation, 56, 68, 76, 99, 101, 135, 139
Exclusion, vi–ix, 4, 4n6, 5, 7, 11n18, 24–36, 40, 42, 47–49, 52–54, 63–66, 68, 69, 81, 87, 92, 106, 113, 115, 122, 129, 136, 144, 145, 148
Executive and budgetary support, 88, 90–91
Experimentalist design, 116
Explicit exclusion, 27–28, 65n6
Extended periods of time, 36
Extermination, 30

F
Farmland, 29
"Fight-flight response," 45
Flawed, 31
Forests, v, 29, 124
Fostering a culture of inclusion, 14
Framework for radical inclusion, 20

Freak-shows, 28
Full participation, ix, 2, 51, 148
Fund, 13n21, 36, 65, 76n18
Funding, 35, 36, 82, 117, 135, 147, 149, 150
Future needs, 25
Future of cities, 13, 98, 113, 118

G
Gainful employment, 28
Garden City, 26, 28–29
Gardens, 15, 15n23, 16, 28, 31, 123
Gender, 5, 42, 44, 51, 100, 115, 126, 139
    responsive community, 100
Gene sequencing, 119
Gentrification, 31
Geographical location, 42
GIS data, 120
Governance, vii, xiii, xiv, 12, 13, 55, 63, 76, 80, 87, 88, 91, 95, 101, 105, 113, 117, 127–130, 135, 151
    by design, 19, 116
    models, 12, 13, 105, 149
Grassroots movements, 42
Green and blue spaces, 15–19, 34
Green bonds, 117
Green building design, 104
Green corridors, 15, 141
Green spaces, 15–17, 34, 34n9, 79
Guest rooms, 33
Guidelines, 32, 32n8, 33, 67, 74, 80, 102, 107, 144

H
Health, viin7, 3, 6, 9n17, 15, 19, 29, 42, 42n7, 44, 49, 65n7, 66, 68, 70, 71, 71n11, 72n12, 73–75, 77, 81, 95, 100, 102, 117, 124, 138, 140, 145

The High Line, 16–17
Homes for the poor, 28
Homophobia, 50
Houseless people with disabilities, 51
Housing, vi, 4, 6, 24n1, 29, 46, 63, 78, 100, 103, 112, 121, 128–130, 146n5, 148
Human agency, 7, 42, 47, 52, 54, 63–65, 81
Human rights, viii, 4, 8, 25, 47, 48, 70, 74, 78, 80, 96, 106, 122, 134, 136, 144
Human-rights based regulatory frameworks, 144
Hurricane Sandy, 137, 138

I
Iceberg of Inequality, x, 94–95
Iceberg of Inequality Model, 87, 94
Ideal citizen, 31
Imaginary cities, 63–67
Immigrants with disabilities, 51
Impairment, vii, 3, 3n1, 5, 10, 33, 44, 47, 102, 118, 120, 141
Implicit bias, 6, 44–46
Implicit exclusion, 28–29
Imrie, Robert, 27, 29–31
Inaccessible, vi, vii, 3, 6, 9, 25–27, 29–31, 65, 99
  cities, 25
  design, 29
  workplaces, 27, 31
Incarcerated people with disabilities, 51
Inclusion efforts, 41
Inclusion imperative, 3, 12
Inclusive, vi–x, viin7, xiii, xiv, 2, 5–8, 11–14, 19, 20, 26, 30, 30n7, 33, 35, 41, 48–51, 54–56, 66–68, 72, 73, 76, 80–82, 86–108, 113, 115–118, 120–122, 124, 126, 129, 130, 134, 136, 140, 143, 146–151
  approach, x, 2, 11–13, 35, 80, 87, 101, 116, 145, 151
  decision-making, 91, 92
  design, 7, 9n17, 11
  development, 2–4, 126
  environments, 32, 34, 82, 101, 120
  public engagement, 35
  society, 25, 91, 107
  spaces, x–xii, 19, 118, 126, 129
  theories, 41
  urban governance models, 12
  urban planning, 91
Inclusive, just, and equitable society, 41
Inclusivity, 20, 46, 57, 81, 86, 88, 108, 112, 134, 135, 141, 144, 148, 149
Independent Living Movement, 40n2, 43, 52
Inequality, xiii, 5, 6n14, 12, 24n1, 31, 48, 50, 64, 74, 77, 81, 87, 100, 122, 129, 134, 151
Influence, 44, 67–68, 89, 90, 92, 127
Information accessibility, 70, 104, 108
Information resources, 33, 135, 149
Infrastructure, viii, 4, 6, 11, 13, 34, 35, 65, 67–69, 72, 79, 82, 103, 104, 107, 118, 122–124, 126, 129, 136, 137, 139–142, 147, 148, 150
Innovative solutions, 6, 19
Insane asylums, 29
Institutional barriers, v
Institutional capacity, 91
Institutionalization, 28, 29
Institutional segregation, 29
Insurance coverage, 35
Integrated solutions, 19
Internet of Things (IoT), 4, 120–123
Intersectionality, 50n17

J
Jail time, 28
Judgments, 44
Jumeirah, 86
Justice, viii, ix, 2, 5n9, 5n10, 6, 6n14, 24, 26, 26n3, 27, 30, 41–44, 46–47, 49–53, 50n17, 64, 81, 105
Justice-oriented social movements, 42

L
Lawsuit, 20, 36
Lawyers, 36
Leave No One Behind (LNOB) principle, 106
Legislation, 36, 43, 70, 91, 105, 107
Limbic system, 45
Lincoln, 27
The Line, 142, 143
Livability, 19, 46, 112
Lived experiences, viii, xiii, 24, 34, 48, 76, 97, 118
Local governments, 12, 24, 24n1, 57, 75, 76, 80, 92, 101, 145, 146
Long Beach, Calif., 36
Los Angeles, 36, 71, 146n5, 150

M
Machine learning (ML), 4, 120, 123, 127, 141
Maimed, 27
Mainstream disability rights programs and policies, 105
Mandatory fine, 28
Marginalization, viii, ix, 20, 30, 51, 64, 106, 115
Marginalized communities, vin3, viii, xiii, xiv, 13, 14, 56
Marginal status, 30
Material deprivation, 30
Measurable goals, 56
Medical abnormality, 43
Medicalization, 30
Medical model, 43
Mental health, 15, 33–36, 100, 137 clinics, 35
Mental wellbeing, 35
Micro mobility solutions, 43
Micro mobility vehicles, 42
Migration flows, 12
Misconceptions, 6
Mismatch, 6–8, 11
Mobility challenges, vii, 36
Mobility-limiting conditions, 36
Mohammed bin Rashid school of government, 86
Moral values, 26
Multiple dimensions of exclusion, 20, 94
Mutilated, 27

N
Nanotechnology, 119
National governments, 12, 98, 99n16, 101, 147
National Inclusive Mobility Strategy, 141
National Municipal Institute of People with Disabilities (IMPD), 40, 139
Natural land, 28
Neoliberalism, 48
NEOM Saudi Arabia, 142–143
Neural systems, 44
Neurodiverse, 15, 31–33
Neurodiversity, 134n1
New Orleans, 27
New Urban Agenda (NUA), 97–101, 99n16, 99n18, 106
New York, 62, 74, 99n18, 137–138, 146n5, 149
New York City, 16–17, 62, 71, 78, 137, 138

Next chapter, 20, 36, 56, 81
Non-disabled people, 31, 74
Normative built environment, 30
Normative ideal, 25
Nuanced approach, ix, 141

O

Older persons, viii, 9, 15, 20, 40, 43, 48, 53, 66, 67, 70, 71, 74, 75, 79, 80, 96, 97, 106, 138
Omaha, 27
Open data, 120
Oppression, 29–31, 50, 51
Orphaned, 29
Othering, ix
Othering & Belonging Institute, 114
Outdated laws, 6
Outdoor spaces, 32, 79
Outliers, 12

P

Pandemics, 3, 41, 49, 66, 70–80, 97, 134, 136–140, 146
Parks, 15, 15n23, 16, 28, 30, 34, 68, 102, 129, 138
Participation, ix, 2, 3n1, 9n17, 30, 47–49, 51, 53, 54, 65, 70, 71, 75, 88–91, 98n13, 99, 106, 124, 145, 148
  barriers, 6
  of the targeted group, 91–92
Participatory forms, 42
Participatory planning, 11, 68–70, 99, 100, 148
Pedestrian crossings, 34
Pennsylvania, 27
People of Determination, 105
People with autism, 31–33, 32n8
People with disabilities, vi, 3n1, 4, 4n6, 7, 26–31, 36, 40, 40n1, 40n2, 43, 46–52, 64, 73, 74, 80, 105, 108, 117, 120, 121, 124, 129, 137, 140, 146n5
Perceptions, 44, 93, 116, 145
Periphery, 28
Personal tragedy models, 43
Persons with disabilities, vii–ix, 3–5, 3n1, 3n5, 11, 15, 20, 28, 30, 31, 45, 48, 52, 53, 57, 64, 65n6, 66, 67, 70, 71, 73–82, 87, 90, 92–94, 97, 98, 102, 106, 113, 114n1, 117, 119n6, 125, 137–139
Physical activity, 15, 19
Physical barriers, v, 51, 64, 107
Physical design changes, 34
Physical environment, 3, 44
Physical inertia, 30
Physical space, 9, 43, 100
Physical wellbeing, 35
Piloting new practices, 12
Planetizen, 36
Plants, 34, 112
Police, 27, 81
Policies, vii–x, xiii, xiv, 4, 12–14, 24, 24n1, 25, 34, 40, 41, 47, 49, 51, 53–55, 64, 65, 67, 69, 70, 74, 76, 80, 87–97, 99, 99n16, 101, 105–107, 114–116, 122, 124, 126, 129, 136, 139, 145, 146, 148, 150, 151
  barriers, 51
PolicyLink, 53
Policymakers, viii, xiv, 6, 11, 12, 14, 45, 55, 113, 126, 127, 144, 145
Politics of difference, 26, 30
Poor work abilities, 31
Population limit, 29
Portland, Ore., 15n23, 27, 36
Post-traumatic stress disorder (PTSD), 34
Poverty, 5, 6n14, 48, 52, 74, 78, 119n6
  rates, 3

Practical opportunities, 5
Prejudice, 6, 30, 44
Programs, ix, 12, 34, 35, 40, 41, 65, 67, 68, 73, 76, 81, 91, 93, 94, 99n18, 100, 101, 105–107, 115, 116, 123, 124, 126, 135, 137, 140, 141, 145–147, 150
The Promenade Plantée, 15
Promoting physical activity, 34
Protected bike lane designs, 20
Providing data, 14
Public gaze, 28
Public health, 19, 75
Public parks, 16, 29, 81
Public planning processes, 20
Public-private initiatives, 43
Public spaces, vi, 9, 17, 28, 30–35, 40, 46, 56, 57, 76, 112, 120, 123, 128, 129, 139, 148
Public transit, 30, 103, 127
Public transport, 27, 139
Public transportation, 6, 32, 65, 86, 97, 118, 120, 121, 127
systems, 6, 31, 112

Q
Quantum computing, 119
Queers with disabilities, 51
Quiet carriages, 35
Quiet rooms, 32
Quito, 141, 149
Quito Listo program, 141

R
Race, 24, 25, 42, 44, 51, 54, 115, 144
Racial inequalities, 24n1
Racial tensions, 31
Racism, 50
Radial communities, 28, 29
Radially planned, 28
Radical inclusion, viii, ix, xiii, xiv, 2–20, 26, 36, 40–57, 63, 64, 66, 80, 81, 87, 88, 95, 101, 114, 118, 120, 121, 136, 144–147, 149–151
and barriers, 2
in cities, 66
and disability justice, 49–51
and spatial justice, ix, 41–47
to understand human agency, 52
in urban planning, 56
for urban transformation, 2–20, 51–54
Radically inclusive cities, x, 7, 11, 30, 49, 66, 81, 86–108, 113
Rain gardens, 15, 15n23
Rapid urbanization, 4, 12, 49
Real-time information, 120, 123
Recreation, 17, 19, 67
opportunities, 15, 79
Redlining, 24n1, 27, 31
Regime change, 31
Regulatory barriers, 51
Reno, 27
Reproducing, 30
Requirements and standards, 6
Reservoirs, 29
Resilience, xiii, 2, 19, 55, 75, 80, 88, 97, 103–104, 106, 128, 134, 136, 141, 144–148, 151
Resilient, 13, 26, 46, 51, 55, 56, 65n7, 66, 73, 79, 87, 100, 112, 117, 134, 136, 144, 149, 150
cities, 114
Restrooms, 7, 34
Retrofit, 34, 65, 68, 104
Rights, viii, 19, 24–26, 29, 40n1, 46, 47, 49–51, 50n17, 53, 64–66, 75, 78, 94, 100, 106, 107, 121, 126, 134
Risk and uncertainty, 13
Risk mitigation, 69

Roberts, Ed, 29, 40, 40n2
Robotics, 119, 122
Robust, 13, 94, 98, 134
Routine repairs, 31

S
Safe routes to school, 34
Safe spaces, 15
San Francisco, 27, 146n5
San Francisco Lighthouse for the Blind, 118
Scaling successful approaches, 12
Schweik, Susan, 27–29
Seating areas, 17, 34
Secure bike parking, 35
Segregation, 24n1, 25, 28, 29, 65n6, 129
Sense of othering, 26
Sensory aids, 33
Sensory garden, 31, 32
Sensory-friendly features, 33
Sensory-friendly public spaces, 32, 35
Sensory processing issues, 32
Service providers, 6, 12, 126
Sexism, 50
Sidewalks, 9, 15n23, 36, 66, 103, 139
Singapore, 139–140
Skills mismatches, 6
Small towns, 28
Smart cities, vi, xiii, 65, 112, 123, 130, 137–144
Smart Dubai Agency, 107
Smart homes, 120
Smart mobility, 118
Social activism, 42
Social and physical positioning, 24
Social attitudes, 6, 122
Social barriers, 107
Social change, vii, 5, 11, 40
Social cohesion, 19, 41, 56
Social construct, 5, 89, 90
Social contract, ix, 31, 41, 44, 46, 62
Social engagement, 15
Social exclusion, 54, 106, 136
Social inclusion, 4, 33, 103–106, 136
Social infrastructure, 148
Social interaction, 19, 33, 71, 103, 145
Socialization, 44
Social justice, viii, 2, 5n9, 6, 6n14, 30, 41, 42, 50, 53
Social relations, 42
Social skills training, 33
Social transformation, 113
Societal beliefs, 27
Societal definitions, 27, 31
Socio-economic inequalities, 31
Socio-institutional beliefs, 31
Socio-political zeitgeist, 31
Solutions, 6, 12, 19, 20, 35, 43, 44, 48, 54, 70, 81, 82, 88, 124, 130
Spaces, viii, x, 9, 10, 15–19, 26, 28, 30, 32, 32n8, 34–36, 34n9, 41–44, 52, 57, 68, 69, 79, 86, 101, 102, 118, 124–126, 146
Spatial, 41–44, 52, 62, 71n11, 100, 124
Spatial dimension, 31, 42, 43
Spatial injustice, 42
Spatial justice, 6, 26n3, 40–47, 52
Spatial segregation, 6
Special accommodations, 48
Speech recognition, 120
Staff training, 14, 33
Stakeholders, vii, ix, xiv, 11, 14, 20, 52, 55, 56, 67, 70, 75, 76, 87, 88, 91, 94, 97, 98n13, 99, 101, 105, 113, 115, 124, 125, 135, 138, 145, 148–151
Standards, 3, 12, 25, 32, 42, 48, 64, 67–70, 98, 101–104, 106, 107, 118, 120n7, 122, 125, 142–144, 147

Stereotypes, 44, 89
Sterilization, 29
Stigma, 24, 30, 49, 73, 75, 96
Stormwater runoff, 15
Streets, 15n23, 27, 29, 36, 40, 47, 64, 76–78, 86, 102, 103, 112, 130, 139
  layout, 28
Structural oppression, 26
Subcortical structure, 45
Suburbanization, 31
Suburban living, 28
Support groups, 35
Sustainable Development Goals (SDGs), 3, 3n5, 12, 52, 99n16, 105, 106, 126
Sustainable future, 105
Sympathy, 27, 28, 45
Systematic barriers, 6
Systems and barriers, 25

T
Targeted policies, 30, 74
Targeted universalism, 53–54, 112–130
Technological transformation, 49
Technology-driven transformation, 113, 121–122
Telehealth services, 35
Ten Principles, 48
Theories and approaches, 20
Trans and gender non-conforming people with disabilities, 51
Transformative interventions, 13
Translation services, 35
Transportation, vi, 4, 25, 28, 32–35, 42n9, 67, 77, 78, 81, 86, 97, 102–103, 105, 117, 118, 123, 124, 127, 128, 138, 141, 142, 148
Transportation infrastructure, 34
Transport systems, 27, 123, 139, 142
Treating all people the same, 30
2030 Agenda, 12

U
UAE disability national strategy, 106
Ugly laws, 26–29
UN Convention on the Rights of Persons with Disabilities (UNCRPD), vii, 3n1, 105–107
Unequal results, 30
UN-Habitat, 62
Unintentionally exclude, 26, 31–36
United Arab Emirates (UAE), 87, 104–107, 140
Universal access, 100
Universal Design, xiv, 7–12, 13n20, 49, 67, 99, 104, 106, 118, 125, 140, 145, 147
Universalist approaches, 114, 115
Unlocking capabilities, 4–7
Unsightly beggar ordinance, 27
Urban agriculture, 15
Urban development, vi, vin3, vii, viin7, x, xiv, 11, 42, 69, 88, 92, 99, 99n16, 105, 106, 122, 124
Urban heat island effect, 15, 123
Urban landscape, 9, 27
Urban planning, vi, xiii, 6, 15, 19, 25, 33–36, 42, 47, 52, 54, 56, 64, 70, 75, 81, 88, 91, 99, 123, 127–130
  and design, vi, 13, 113, 114
Urbanization, ix, 4, 12, 26, 29, 49, 63, 65, 66, 70, 71, 81, 87, 99n16, 101, 105, 106
Urban transformation, vi, 2–20, 41, 51–54, 80, 136–137, 140, 147–151
Usability, 9, 67, 69, 144
U.S. cities, 36

Use of social life, 30
Utopian city, 26
Utopian ideal, 28

V
Vagrants, 28
Valuable 500, 108
Varanasi, 42
Virtual Reality (VR), 34, 120
Vision of leadership, 104
Visual distractions, 32
Visual fire alarms, 33

W
Water fountains, 34
Waterways, 15, 17, 34n9
Wayfinding tools, 33
Weighted blankets, 33
Welcoming spaces, 19

Wellbeing, xiii, 7, 9, 15, 19, 29, 35, 47, 56, 64, 71, 81, 124, 128, 129
Well-maintained networks, 36
Wheelchair-accessible rooms, 33
Wheelchair-friendly, 117
White noise machines, 33
WHO Age Friendly Cities and Communities frameworks, 106
Whole-of-government approach, 96
Whole-of-society approach, 96
Workplaces, 56, 64, 68, 81, 103

Y
Yemen, 42
Young, Iris Marion, 26, 27, 29–31

Z
Zeitgeist, 31, 90, 91
Zip Code, 42, 42n7

SPRINGER NATURE

GPSR Compliance

The European Union's (EU) General Product Safety Regulation (GPSR) is a set of rules that requires consumer products to be safe and our obligations to ensure this.

If you have any concerns about our products, you can contact us on ProductSafety@springernature.com

In case Publisher is established outside the EU, the EU authorized representative is:

Springer Nature Customer Service Center GmbH
Europaplatz 3
69115 Heidelberg, Germany

The manufacturer's authorised representative in the EU is Springer Nature Customer Service Centre GmbH, Europaplatz 3, 69115 Heidelberg, Germany. If you have any concerns regarding our products, please contact ProductSafety@springernature.com

Printed and bound by CPI Group (UK) Ltd, Croydon, CR0 4YY
25/03/2026
02078175-0001